Small Church,
Excellent Ministry

Small Church, Excellent Ministry

A Guidebook for Pastors

EDITED BY
JEFFREY C. FARMER

Foreword by
Karl Vaters

Preface by
Frank Page

WIPF & STOCK · Eugene, Oregon

SMALL CHURCH, EXCELLENT MINISTRY
A Guidebook for Pastors

Wipf & Stock
An Imprint of Wipf and Stock Publishers
199 W. 8th Ave., Suite 3
Eugene, OR 97401

www.wipfandstock.com

PAPERBACK ISBN: 978-1-4982-9886-5
HARDCOVER ISBN: 978-1-4982-9888-9
EBOOK ISBN: 978-1-4982-9887-2

Manufactured in the U.S.A.   DECEMBER 15, 2017

I dedicate this book to my wife, Karen.
God has blessed me with the best.

I would like to thank my colleagues at New Orleans Baptist
Theological Seminary for the hard work they have invested in this
book. Their love for Christ and his ministers of small churches is
evident in the work presented here.

Contents

CONTENTS

List of Authors

Page Brooks, Senior Pastor, Canal Street Church: A Mosaic Community, Founder and President of The Restoration Initiative for Culture and Community, a community development ministry, Associate Professor of Theology and Culture, New Orleans Baptist Theological Seminary.

Jody Dean, Assistant Professor for Christian Education, Director, Mentoring Programs in Christian Education, New Orleans Baptist Theological Seminary.

Jeffrey Farmer, Associate Professor of Church Ministry and Evangelism, Associate Director of the Caskey Center for Church Excellence, New Orleans Baptist Theological Seminary.

Adam Hughes, Dean of Chapel and Director of The Adrian Rogers Center for Expository Preaching, Assistant Professor of Expository Preaching, Director, Mentoring Programs in Pastoral Ministries, New Orleans Baptist Theological Seminary.

Bo Rice, Associate Dean of Supervised Ministry and Mentoring Programs, Assistant Professor of Evangelism and Preaching, New Orleans Baptist Theological Seminary.

Jake Roudkovski, Director, Doctor of Ministry Program, Professor of Evangelism and Pastoral Leadership occupying the Max and Bonnie Thornhill Chair of Evangelism, New Orleans Baptist Theological Seminary.

LIST OF AUTHORS

Ed Steele, Professor of Music, Leavell College, New Orleans Baptist Theological Seminary.

Ed Stetzer, The Billy Graham Distinguished Chair of Church, Mission, and Evangelism, Executive Director, Billy Graham Center for Evangelism, Wheaton College, Wheaton, Illinois.

Hal Stewart, Associate Professor of Discipleship, occupying the Broadmoor Chair of Discipleship, Director of Spiritual Formation, Director of the Doctor of Education Degree Program, New Orleans Baptist Theological Seminary.

Mark Tolbert, Professor of Preaching and Pastoral Ministry, Director, Caskey Center for Church Excellence, occupying the Caskey Chair of Church Excellence, New Orleans Baptist Theological Seminary.

Patrick Weaver, Research Fellow, Caskey Center for Church Excellence, New Orleans Baptist Theological Seminary.

Foreword

Karl Vater

Have you ever tried to find something, but missed it, not because it was tucked away in a long-forgotten corner, but because it was so obvious you'd gotten used to overlooking it?

Small churches are like that.

Looking for the key to revival? In the places where the church is growing as a percentage of the population, it's happening mostly through the multiplication of small churches.

Wondering where the church leaders of tomorrow are? Small churches have been, and remain, the primary training ground for young ministers.

Concerned about a world splintered by race, politics, age, denomination, socioeconomic status, and more? All over the world, men and women of all ages, races, denominations, political backgrounds, and incomes gather together in small congregations to worship Jesus.

No, the church isn't perfect. And neither is the small church.

We're as susceptible to pettiness, jealousy, and infighting as any other group, because we're made up of people too. But that shouldn't surprise us. The church has always had people problems. Most of the New Testament letters were written to address and correct those errors. But, despite those imperfections, mistakes, and sins, Jesus used the small congregations of the early church to change the world.

And he's still doing it today. One person at a time, one family at a time, one community at a time. In small towns and big cities, small churches are still how over half the Christians in the world choose to worship Jesus.[1]

But most of us continue to overlook that reality, including the people who worship in, and (far too often) the people who pastor, small churches. Instead of seeing and leveraging the extraordinary blessings of the small church, we often overlook, complain, and sometimes despise the very churches that are blessing us.

For that reason, small churches may be the most under-resourced aspect of the body of Christ. There are great books, blogs, videos, conferences, and seminary classes about how to break growth barriers. Pastors of large- and megachurches are very generous about sharing the lessons they're learning about how to do better ministry. But they do it from their context—a big church context—because that's the water they're swimming in.

So who's helping small-church pastors lead our churches well *before* we break through those growth barriers? Or to stop seeing smallness not as a barrier to overcome, but as a strategic advantage that Christ wants to use? What does a healthy small church even look like? I've asked that question to thousands of pastors, and have usually been met with blank stares.

Too often, we're unable to see the values inherent in the most common expression of the body of Christ—the small churches of the world. It's time to stop overlooking that and start shining a light on it.

Big and megachurches are great! How can we not rejoice when, say, 5,000 people gather in one place to worship Jesus? That's something to celebrate and thank God for. But it's also great when 5,000 people are worshipping Jesus scattered among 100 different congregations, from multiple denominations in every corner of the city.

I wouldn't want to go back to a world without big churches and the blessings they provide. But we're long overdue to start appreciating, resourcing, and being grateful for the other half—the too-long-overlooked half—of the body of Christ: the small church.

That's why I'm so grateful for the book you're reading right now. Jeffrey Farmer has assembled some great church leaders to help us turn our attention back to this valuable, but overlooked segment of the church. To

---

1. According to the 2014 National Congregations Study, a little more than half the population of the United States attend churches with less than 250 in worship. Bell, "What is an 'Average Church?,'" n.p.

encourage and resource small-church pastors like us with practical, usable information for small churches everywhere.

There's so much we can learn from each other. And so much we need to know about how to minister in and from the small church. Let's get started.

BIBLIOGRAPHY

Bell, Michael. "What is an 'Average Church?,'" http://www.internetmonk.com/archive/michael-bell-what-is-an-average-church.

Preface

FRANK PAGE,
CEO OF SBC EXECUTIVE COMMITTEE

My first pastorate was the First Baptist Church of Possum Kingdom Lake, Texas. Yes, that is the name! This rural church is about seventy-five miles west of Fort Worth. At the grand old age of twenty-six, I became the full-time pastor of that small church. Having experienced a split, it was a church in need of pastoring and leadership. The truth is that I learned more from that situation and gathered more experience than in any other pastorate. I hope I was a blessing to them. The little church grew and we worked through a building program to build a new sanctuary. Fortunately, we were able to pay for it with cash. I developed relationships there that I maintained for decades. While we had some difficult days, by and large it was a wonderful pastorate with supportive people. My first daughter was born while pastoring that open-country church in West Central Texas. One could not see a human habitation from the church house as far as the eye could see. There was far more cattle than there were people in that area. However, God blessed us with people coming to Christ and the church doubled in attendance in my tenure.

Small churches make up the vast majority of our Southern Baptist constituency. Exact numbers can be debated, but the truth is that out of our 47,000-plus churches, close to 40,000 average less than 100 people in attendance.[2]

Of the approximately 47,000 churches of the Southern Baptist Convention, only 169 average over 2,000 members.[3] As I like to tease, that comes from letting the preachers count! The reality is the vast majority of Southern Baptist churches and the vast majority of evangelical churches are small in membership size. However, their size allows for mutual accountability and fellowship that is profound and special.

The majority of Southern Baptist churches are also bivocational. In some of our states, the percentage of bivocational pastors is 80 percent or higher. Those pastors juggle family, secular work, and ministry work. They are the true heroes of our day. Praise God for pastors who serve in those settings.

I am a big fan of smaller-membership and bivocational churches. I spend much of my time traveling and encouraging those churches and pastors. I pray that this book will be a great encouragement as we recognize the excellent ministry that is found in smaller-membership churches. May God bless these true heroes!

In this new book, *Small Church, Excellent Ministry: A Guidebook for Pastors*, you will read many stories which will be an encouragement. You will hear different perspectives of how to make smaller-membership churches truly effective. You will read from various ethnic perspectives and acquire new viewpoints. This is a highly practical book and it will help in how to do the work of the ministry, lead the work of the ministry, and expand the work of the ministry. I am grateful to Dr. Farmer and all of the contributors as they have worked diligently to provide a resource which is specifically focused on the vast number of churches in evangelicalism.

---

2. Based on 2016 Annual Church Profile statistics of the Southern Baptist Convention.

3. Ibid.

Introduction

Jeffrey Farmer

In 1981, Joe Cothen published his pastor's handbook, *Equipped for Good Work: A Guide for Pastors,* and he began his preface by saying, "'The pastor is the key' . . . the man of God in the local church is told that he is the person who can get things done."[4] This statement reflects the importance of being equipped to serve as pastor. With the current trend of decline in Evangelical churches in the United States, this need is even more alarming. Estimates of the population of evangelicals in the United States range from 13.1 percent to 25 percent, though the more accurate projection is probably closer to the lower end of the range.

If you are reading this book, it is probably a safe assumption that you are either currently serving as a pastor or are called to be a pastor. Odds are very good that you are now pastoring or soon will be pastoring a smaller-membership church. This is a great thing! Historically, small churches have made a big impact on the world. They have been around from the beginning of the church at Pentecost, and will be present until the return of Jesus Christ. Small churches are normal churches.

So what do I mean when I say that small churches are normal churches? Quite simply, I mean that the average church is a small church. Using statistics from the Southern Baptist Convention's (SBC) 2015 Annual Church

4. Cothen, *Equipped for Good Work: A Guide for Pastors,* xiv.

Profile, there were 39,421 SBC churches.[5] Of these, there were 24,098 churches with an average weekly worship attendance of less than 100.[6] This means 61 percent of all SBC churches have less than one hundred in weekly worship attendance. Furthermore, 4,742 SBC churches are between 100 and 150 in weekly worship attendance.[7] This means that 28,840 SBC churches have 150 or less in weekly worship attendance. This is 74 percent of the SBC churches. A total of 2,111 churches average a worship attendance between 150 and 200 each week, and a total of 1,229 churches average between 200 and 250 each week. Simple calculations reveal that smaller-membership churches (250 or less in Average Worship Attendance) account for 81.6 percent of the Southern Baptist Convention.

This does not mean that God does not use larger churches for the Kingdom work. Quite the contrary, 54 percent of the Cooperative Program giving and approximately half of the total baptisms came from larger churches.[8] This book is definitely not hostile toward those serving in larger churches. Instead, we acknowledge the subtleties and nuances required for serving effectively in smaller churches.

I serve as the Associate Director of the Caskey Center for Church Excellence at New Orleans Baptist Theological Seminary. The Caskey Center exists to provide resources for pastors serving in smaller-membership churches so they can conduct their ministry with excellence. Prior to serving with the Caskey Center, I was a church planter of a network of small, organic churches (some people would call these house churches), and prior to that, I served in various ministry positions in both small and large churches. Over the years, I have learned the value of smaller-church ministry, and some of the limitations.

Ministering with excellence in a smaller-membership church requires commitment, intentionality, and perseverance. It also requires the pastor to equip and mobilize the church members for ministry while also maintaining close relationships with as many members as possible. In short, the small church pastor must be a mix of General James Mattis and Sheriff Andy Taylor.

The purpose of this book is to equip ministers serving the small church with the necessary tools to perform their ministries with excellence.

5. Based on 2015 Annual Church Profile statistics of the Southern Baptist Convention.
6. Ibid.
7. Ibid.
8. Ibid.

There are four sections of this book. The first section deals with ministry settings. We examine two keys for effective small-church ministry—being on mission and multiethnic ministry. The second section addresses pastoral ministry in the small church. These include evangelism, preaching, and worship leadership. The third section focuses on discipleship and Christian education issues for the small church. Chapters address leadership, administration, and discipleship for the small-church pastor. The final section focuses on the pastor's personal life. This includes the pastor's personal spiritual health and the health of the pastor's family.

SECTION 1

Small-Church Ministry Settings

1

Getting Small Churches on Mission

ED STETZER

As the people of a missionary God, we are entrusted to participate in the world the same way he does—by committing to be his ambassadors (see John 20:21; 2 Cor 5:20). "Missional" describes the perspective to see people as God does and to engage in the activity of reaching them. The church on mission is the church as God intended, loving our neighbors as ourselves, and proclaiming the good news of redemption found in Jesus.

SMALL MATTERS IN MISSION

In today's church culture, we seem to focus a larger percentage of our writings, thoughts, and conferences on larger churches and how they are reaching people for Jesus. Their pastors seem to be the go-to public figures for speaking invitations, and their model(s) of church growth are extolled as something for all churches to emulate. But while there are many reasons to celebrate the things larger churches have already done (and continue to accomplish), sometimes we fail to overlook (at best) and neglect (at worst) the work that small churches can do and are doing. Small churches (250 or less members/attenders) make up the vast majority of evangelical churches in the United States.

Popular pastor and author Francis Chan left a church he and his wife had founded, a church that had grown to over 5,000 in its seven years of existence. Recently he went into detail on why he left:

> "I got frustrated at a point, just biblically. According to the Bible, every single one of these people has a supernatural gift that's meant to be used for the body. And I'm like 5,000 people show up every week to hear my gift, see my gift. That's a lot of waste. Then I started thinking how much does it cost to run this thing? Millions of dollars! So I'm wasting the human resource of these people that according to Scripture have a miraculous gift that they could contribute to the body but they're just sitting there quietly. . . . [T]hey just sit there and listen to me."[1]

Today, Chan leads a small house church network in San Francisco called We Are Church.[2] Chan disciples leaders in the network, two pastors per house church who work for free, and enjoys this smaller setting where everyone can make use of their spiritual gifts. Everyone reads the Bible for themselves. Chan does not preach. They meet in homes and pray and care for one another. The plan is to double the number of house churches every year so that in ten years, there would be over a million people committed to actively being the church.[3]

Chan's theology of gifting and service in the church is supported by Paul's writings in 1 Corinthians 12. Paul makes note that God gives spiritual gifts to each believer, and that believers are to work together for the good of the church. He immediately moves to the unity of the church and makes special note that members working together, exercising their gifts and not letting the supposedly more important gifts take center stage, leads to a healthy church. In Chan's mind, it is difficult in a large church for each member to exercise his or her gift. The point is movement, which can happen in larger churches, but is essential in smaller churches.

In addition to churches, large and small, understanding the giftings of their members, all churches need to begin with an understanding of their identity as a church. The concept of sentness is critical to an accurate biblical understanding of the church and its relationship to the world.

---

1. Lynn, "Francis Chan Goes Into Detail," para. 3.
2. www.wearechurch.com.
3. Lynn, "Francis Chan Goes Into Detail," para. 17.

BIG PICTURE FOR SMALLER CHURCHES

Many people sit in small churches each week and wonder how to move forward. Let me suggest several big-picture ways to begin moving toward mission and then in the remainder of the chapter iterate ten very practical applications

Develop a Global Vision

The church was created to be God's witness to the ends of the Earth (Acts 1:8). Too many churches use this verse as a missions strategy, beginning in their own Jerusalem (their own town), and then moving to Samaria (the surrounding region or the US in general), and then to the ends of the earth (overseas missions). There are several issues with this line of thinking. First, the point of the verse, and the book of Acts as a whole, and the whole Bible for that matter, is for the gospel to get to the ends of the earth. Second, there is a danger of focusing too much on our own "Jerusalems" to the point that there is nothing left—no money and no people—to send to the ends of the earth. Third, this thinking can leave missional engagement to someone else because it is not the first priority of the church.

David Platt stated in his book, *Radical*, that he felt a disconnect between following Jesus, who focused on a small group of churches, and pastoring a megachurch.[4] Yet, God put him in a megachurch for a time. Platt essentially reversed the geographic focus of Acts 1:8. He made global engagement the first priority and believed that mobilizing the majority of resources for the ends of the earth would result in a trickle-down effect to national and local engagement. People with a global vision see their own community in a different light because they own mission and take personal responsibility for the Great Commission.

How can a small church grow its global vision? Be in touch with global trends in missions.[5] Be informed through relationships with missionaries on the field. Denominations typically can provide a listing of their missionaries along with prayer points for each. Contact a reputable

---

4. Platt, *Radical*, 1-2.

5. Two recent books are essential reading: J.D. Payne, *Pressure Points: Twelve Global Issues Shaping the Face of the Church* (Thomas Nelson, 2013) and David Sills, *Changing World, Unchanging Mission: Responding to Global Challenges* (IVP, 2015).

mission agency and sign up for their prayer letters.[6] Hearing regular reports from those in the field brings a vitality to a local church. Finally, take personal responsibility for the Great Commission. Jesus commissioned the church, and all churches (Matt 28:19–20). The Great Commission is for everyone. Everyone can pray, give, go, or welcome those who have come here. Churches who take this seriously are typically churches ready to move globally and locally.

Pray Strategically

Do you really believe Jesus when he said "The harvest is plentiful, but the laborers are few. Therefore pray earnestly to the Lord of the harvest to send out laborers into his harvest" (Luke 10:2)? Churches who believe this passage will sense an urgency to understand the state of the world and pray strategically for the advance of the gospel. Pray for God to raise up missionaries, church planters, and gospel workers from within your own congregation. Pray and seek ways to give more and to go more. Use prayer resources such as Operation World, peoplegroups.info, the Joshua Project, and the Caleb Project. Get a laminated world map the size of your dinner table and use it in place of a table cloth. You'll be amazed at how often the conversation turns to local and global gospel issues because people are now looking at the world on a regular basis.

Preach Passionately

Simply putting before your church a list of ideas for mission will not result in long-term change. Developing a global vision and praying strategically will begin to replace the inactive bits of DNA in your church with missional DNA. For pastors, preach faithfully through all the Scriptures and don't miss the thread of God's heart for the nations that runs throughout the Bible. The identity of God's people has always been geared toward mission. Let your people see that week after week from the Scripture. The following quote has often been attributed to missionary martyr Jim Elliot, "Why do you need a voice when you have a verse?"

---

6. A list of reputable vetted agencies can be found here: http://www.thetravelingteam. org/agencies.

Lead your people deeply into the Scripture and you'll move them close to God's heart, which is certainly missional.

MISSION IN SMALLER CHURCHES

Numerically, smaller churches dominate US life. They should also be key parts of the mission.

There is much benefit, therefore, in identifying various ways that smaller churches can reach their communities and beyond for Christ. This chapter will identify and briefly expound a few ways small churches can be mission-minded, both locally and globally. They are in no particular order of preference or importance, and there is certainly no expectation that a church on mission would only select one of these opportunities. Many coalesce together and can be seamlessly integrated to form a more fully orbed missional church.

Small Churches can Serve the Hurting and Poor.

Today, churches are known for many things, but meeting the needs of the hurting and poor is rarely (if ever) one of them. If we join Jesus on his mission, I think we too will serve those who are hurting. In fact, I think the world is often confused when they see a church that claims to follow Jesus but is not actually doing much of what Jesus did. They know *he* healed the sick and ministered to the hurting, and they wonder why a church would be unengaged in these areas. To paraphrase Ghandi, "Why do your Christians look so little like your Jesus?"

Think back to the early church. One of the primary activities they were known for was serving the poor. As one Roman emperor, Julian the Apostate, wrote:

> These [*Christians*] not only feed their own, but ours also; welcoming them with their [love], they attract them, as children are attracted with cakes . . . Whilst the pagan priests neglect the poor, the hated [Christians] devote themselves to works of charity, and by a display of false compassion have established and given effect to their pernicious errors. Such practice is common among them, and causes contempt for our gods.[7]

7. Emperor Julian, *Epistle to the Pagan High Priests*. See also Hunter, *To Change the World*, 55-56.

He knew that acts of charity towards the least of society in the name of Jesus were having a profound effect. The marginalized, those who had little to give to society, still had value and worth in the eyes of God and Christians, and as their needs were met their hearts were opened to abandoning false gods and learning about Jesus. Small churches can recapture this passion for ministering to the hurting in their communities. You don't need state-of-the-art worship facilities or a seven-digit church budget to care for those in need. You only need to be willing to engage and empathize with the downcast and weary, and in doing so you might see their hearts opened to Jesus.

Small churches can partner together, either through association via a denominational structure or as part of a city partnership, to pool resources towards this end. A food pantry that is stocked once per month by a different church is an affordable way that small churches can contribute. Giving to a ministerial alliance fund specifically created to assist with an overdue utility bill or missed rent payment means the world to someone on the brink of having their electricity cut off or being evicted from their home.

Some churches have partnered together to pool money in an effort to help the poor out of the vicious cycle of predatory lending and title loan companies. With interest rates often exceeding 400% (and sometimes 4,000%), persons who are at the end of their financial rope are falling prey to such loans not because they lack business savvy but because they have no other option. In the long run, these loans always cost the borrower much more than a regular loan does.

One such example is University Heights Baptist Church in Springfield, Missouri. They partnered with a local credit union, providing $20,000 in seed money, to begin a program of helping those with high-interest loans. Small churches can make a tangible difference in the lives of the poor in their community by helping them get out of debilitating debt. And a person who has been helped in a tangible way is often open to hearing about Jesus.

Small Churches can be on Mission by Helping Members Become Certified as Foster Parents

In many states, foster care workers are overworked, underpaid, and incredibly stressed. In any given year, there are over 400,000 children in the foster system. States are always looking to recruit more certified foster parents. In 2016, multiple states were forced to house children in foster care offices or motels, sometimes for only a day or two but sometimes for weeks at a time. Small churches could easily work towards certifying three to five families in their congregations, which would have an immediate impact in several ways. First, children could be placed in caring homes on their first night instead of in hotels, offices, or already-crowded foster homes. Second, Christian foster homes have a unique opportunity to care both for the physical and spiritual needs of displaced, confused, and hurting children.

In 2016, 60 percent of all children in foster care were non-white.[8] One way churches can become more multiethnic is through foster care. I have a friend who, along with his wife, has been certified as a foster parent for over five years. They have had multiple ethnicities and races in their home and always make a point to bring children in the foster system to church with them. In one instance, their church pooled resources together to help the mother of their foster children. She desperately wanted to regain custody of her children but needed an apartment and furniture before the state would return them to her. After she found an apartment, church members collected couches, beds, and other living necessities and helped to furnish her apartment. It was a holistic effort at ministering to this family, meeting the needs of both the children and the mother. Other instances include parents being invited to church on Sundays so they can see their children in addition to their state-appointed foster care visits (of course this needs to be discussed with the case worker to ensure the safety of the children).

Often, foster care will result in children being reunited with their parents (or a relative). Sometimes, though, children are made available for adoption. Currently there are over 100,000 children in foster care who are eligible for adoption.[9] As James instructs believers, part of living the Christian life is caring for orphans. Not everyone is called to adopt from foster care, or even adopt at all. But we are called to care for orphans, and small churches that are engaged in foster care can minister to children in vulnerable circumstances. What time could be better to tell them of a Father who created and loves them and a Savior who came to be the rescuer?

8. "Foster Care Statistics 2015," 9.
9. Adopt Us Kids, "About the Children," para. 7.

Small Churches can Identify an Unreached People Group or an Unengaged Unreached People Group and Begin Strategizing Ways to Share the Gospel with them.

An unreached people group is defined as a population similar in language and customs that has less than 2 percent of an evangelical presence within its group.[10] According to the International Mission Board, there are currently over 6,700 unreached people groups in the world.[11] Unengaged, unreached people groups are unreached people groups that have no active church planting strategy among them. Currently, there are over 3,000 unengaged, unreached people groups in the world.[12]

Small churches can engage the lost by identifying and beginning to plan ways to minister specifically to one unreached or unengaged, unreached people group. Time in weekly corporate prayer should be devoted to this people group. Members can spend time in daily prayer for the needs of these people. Certainly there are spiritual needs; that is why they are an unreached people group. Pray for Christ to be made known to them. But there are also various physical needs that can be prayed for. These will be unique to each group, but churches that are serious about making Jesus known in all the world will be compelled to pray for wholeness of life.

As with many things, as we become committed in prayer for a certain matter (especially those with spiritual implications), God moves our hearts to do more than pray. I know a pastor of a small church who has begun a partnership with a missions agency. After six months of research and four months of congregational education, his church adopted an unreached people group in West Africa. A few times each year, he and a few others fly over and spend a week hiking from village to village sharing the good news of Jesus. The cost isn't exorbitant ($2,000 round trip per person). In seventeen trips, they have shared the gospel in countless villages and have seen over thirty-five people come to declare Jesus is Lord. They are making a legitimate and successful attempt to push back the darkness and make disciples that will one day worship King Jesus for eternity.

---

10. International Mission Board, "Key Terms," n.p.

11. International Mission Board, https://www.imb.org/topic/explore-missions/missions-and-world-today/lesson-1-unreached-and-unengaged-people-groups, para. 4.

12. Ibid. Missions organizations define terms differently and often have differing numbers. The International Mission Board of the Southern Baptist Convention provides research that is reliable and helpful and so, without denigrating other sources, we list only theirs for general information.

Small Churches can Adopt the Same (or Different) Unengaged, Unreached People Group Currently Living in the United States

In addition to overseas work, consider how you can share the gospel effectively and long-term with a people group in America. States like Oklahoma, Louisiana, North Carolina, and Iowa, to name only a few, have thousands of people who comprise various unengaged, unreached people groups. They are as spiritually destitute and lost as those living overseas without a gospel witness. If your church is geographically near one of these groups, then begin praying about how you can begin a ministry to them. Preach on the value of avoiding worldly wealth and, instead, storing up treasures in heaven in hopes that some of your members will envision themselves selling their homes and moving closer to this group to encounter them daily in their neighborhoods.

These groups, depending on location, are either centralized (think one main neighborhood) or decentralized (think ethnic neighborhood[s] spread throughout a city). But as a people group, they share common languages and customs. Interacting with them in their environment, learning their culture, understanding their traditions and religion(s) will allow you to be better prepared to engage them with the gospel. Befriend them. See them not as a project to be conquered or a task to be checked off the list, but people who are lovable and need to learn about their Creator.

Churches that are willing to pursue both international and national unengaged, unreached people groups could look, for instance, at the Khuen people. There are 3,000 in the San Francisco area and 13,000 in Myanmar (formerly Burma). Churches in or near the Bay Area could interact with US residents first and begin incorporating international trips as well. The cultural similarities, despite the distance of almost 8,000 miles between San Francisco and Myanmar, unite these people much more so than it divides them. Myanmar has a long history of mission work (read about Adoniram Judson and his work in the country in the first half of the 19th century).

Small Churches can Make an Impact Simply by Making their Building(s) Available to Various Constituencies in their Communities.

Typically, small churches use their facilities no more than six hours per week. The other 162 hours of the week buildings sit empty and woefully underused. Open your property to a church plant in need of a place to worship. Invite the local addiction recovery chapter to meet in your building for as long as they want. Offer to provide coffee and cookies baked by a different member each week. Neighborhood association meetings are often looking for a place to hold gatherings. These take place no more than once a month (usually much less frequently) and are a wonderful way to get people to come to your building. Boy Scout and Girl Scout troops are always looking for places to hold weekly meetings. Let your building(s) be a blessing to your community. Value relationships with your neighbors more than you value the cleanliness of the carpet in your sanctuary. Serving people is more important than a pristine fellowship hall. Your community will soon take note of which churches care about them and which churches care only about themselves. Be the former, not the latter.

One of the most successful ways of serving your community is to offer a free night of babysitting so parents can have a date night. Sometimes this is structured around Christmas so parents can shop together without having to bring their kids and hide purchases. Often it is simply a random Friday or Saturday evening where parents can spend an evening strengthening their marriage without shelling out $20–$40 on a babysitter. The kids are served a meal, presented a Bible lesson, and allowed to play together. At pickup, church members tell parents about one unique thing their child(ren) did that night, showing that each child was valued. It is also a time where families can be invited to attend worship the following Sunday. Something as simple as taking down their name, address, or email for the promise of inviting them to future 'Date Night' babysitting events produces a ready-made list of prospects for future contact and evangelism.

In any way that you use your building(s) to serve your community, make sure you have members at each meeting to unlock the facilities and to welcome all who enter. They are there to assist, not to eavesdrop on the meetings. A warm welcome goes a long way towards showing them you really care about them, not simply that you're begrudgingly providing a community service. And it should go without saying, but just so no one misunderstands, all of these opportunities should be rent-free for the users. Don't try to make a buck off of your community. Don't even justify it as covering your costs. Take the hit; pay for the electricity usage out of your own pocket. Some might demand that they pay and that's okay. Just make sure they know you're going to designate the money towards something worthwhile in your community, like funding the food pantry mentioned above. People will appreciate hearing that their gifts aren't going to pay the salaries of church employees.

Provide an Environment where the Arts are Offered to Neighborhood Children

Christianity used to be the epicenter of the arts. The best in music, sculpture, paintings, etc., all flowed from a Christian worldview. This has reversed since the Enlightenment and the church produces very little art, though it is making a revival. With cuts to local school budgets, small churches are primed to lead the way in their communities by offering free (or substantially lower-than-market-rate) piano lessons. The congregational pianist could invest five to ten hours per week tutoring children for a determined period (say an academic school year) and tie continued participation in the program with successful school grades. This gives students incentive to participate and the benefit of learning how to play an instrument.

Churches are also usually able to offer instruction in other artistic venues such as choir or painting. While older children may not find participating in choir appealing, I have yet to meet a younger child (say, under eleven) that doesn't love to sing. A neighborhood kids choir provides children an opportunity to learn how to read music, how to operate in a group, reinforces the discipline needed to memorize words and notes, and offers an environment that celebrates all that is good within the arts. As for painting, children regardless of age love to paint. Churches could provide the supplies and children bring their own canvases, both groups sharing the cost of this ministry. Imagination and the ability to create are God-given blessings that humans can use to glorify Jesus. Small churches can lead in reclaiming the arts towards a Christian focus.

In any and all of these artistic venues, make sure that teachers are linking the beauty of music and art with the Creator God. We celebrate the splendor of nature not because it is an end to itself, but because it points to God (Ps 19:1). Romans 1:20 explains that creation teaches us about God's power and nature. Because we experience creation, we can know some things about him. Therefore, we can teach about God while we use the arts to serve the community.

Small Churches can "Adopt" a Particular Local Group and Consistently Serve Them

This could vary from groups like police or fire departments and EMTs, to the teachers at a particular elementary, middle, or high school, to a retirement home. Having a long-term relationship with a particular group fosters a deeper level of commitment and love than can occur with a one-time service project. The longer you serve this group, the more you will come to know them as persons, the more deeply you will involve yourself in their lives, the more intimately you will know their hurts and needs. Being able to sit with someone who is losing a family member to cancer happens after years of loving service, not because you mowed their lawn once or cleaned the leaves out of their clogged gutters.

Once a year, have a celebration dinner on behalf of your group. Cook a nice meal, have the kids' choir sing the songs they've learned that year (as mentioned above), and honor them for various accomplishments they have achieved in the past year. Create silly awards to pass out, give people a reason to laugh together. Make it an event that they look forward to each year. Show them that they matter, that someone appreciates them for who they are as persons. Make sure the event is saturated in Christian themes, such as love, compassion, and hope. Let them hear with their ears (as they have seen with their eyes throughout the past year) that Jesus loves them.

Small Churches could Develop a Jail Ministry

Local and county jails almost always appreciate any attempt to lower recidivism and the evangelism and discipleship of inmates is a proven way to lower repeat offenses. The United States has the highest incarceration rate in the world with over 2.5 million persons locked up. Of those, approximately 1 million are in city or county jails. Unlike state or federal prisons, those in jail have often not yet been convicted of a crime. They have been charged with an offense (major or minor) and are awaiting trial. Persons convicted of sentences of a year or less often serve out their time in a jail. Jails are a fertile ground for sharing the gospel liberally.

Jail ministry, like all new ministries, must be birthed after a long time of prayer with those who are interested in such a mission. Let the Holy Spirit soften your heart to incarcerated persons. Mediate on Jesus' words in Matthew 25:36–40. When you minister to those in jail, to the least of these, you are ministering unto Jesus himself. After confirming a commitment to this ministry, set up a meeting with the local sheriff or chief of police. A face-to-face meeting is often more effective, allowing you to lay out your plan of weekly ministry. It may be that there is already an evangelical ministry to this jail. See about joining with them or asking for suggestions about nearby jails where no ministry currently exists.

The two components helpful for a fruitful jail ministry are an ample supply of Bibles to hand out to anyone who asks, and a consistent, weekly commitment to show up. The Bibles need to be in a contemporary translation that is easy to understand and the meetings must meet the spiritual needs of the prisoners. There will be a mix of baby believers and unbelievers who show up for Bible study. Make sure to focus on helping them to understand the grand narrative of the Bible: God created a world, humans rebelled, and Jesus' life and death reconciles back to God those who repent and believe in him.

These men or women need to hear that God in Christ loves them. They need to know that they have value and that God has not abandoned them. Also remember that this isn't seminary or even a Bible college. Keep the teaching simple and straightforward. Give them opportunities to contribute. Christians need to grow and unbelievers need a chance to ask legitimate questions without fear of ridicule.

If you are granted access for a ministry, make sure to inquire about any rules or policies that you may not be aware of so you can stay compliant. It is vitally important that you maintain respect towards those who are in charge. Additionally, make sure there are at least two people who lead this ministry. This is beneficial both for a long-term strategy of multiplication and short-term continuity if one leader is sick or on vacation. Jail ministries will not thrive if they are inconsistent. In the same way that Chuck Colson showed that prison ministry can be effective, jail ministry is often an untapped field white unto harvest for those who are willing to do the hard work of tilling and sowing.

Small Churches can Provide After-school tutoring for children in the area.

Research indicates that students who are not reading at grade level by the time they complete third grade are almost always unlikely to ever catch up. In 2009, 68 percent of all fourth graders in public schools were reading below grade level.[13] Students who do not read at grade level are more likely to drop out before earning a diploma and are underprepared to enter the workforce as skilled laborers. Society as a whole, not to mention the individual himself, suffers from illiterate and under-literate citizens.

A semi-structured program where retirees help these students to read better provides an excellent resource for children who need extra help honing their reading and comprehension skills. Even thirty minutes spent with a child each school day working on reading skills will pay incredible dividends. Parents will see results and be grateful for the time spent with their children on a focused activity. Additionally, children will see that coming to a church building can be beneficial for them. Kids want to read, they want to explore the worlds found within books. And church members who commit a little bit of time each day to make their dreams come true can be a catalyst to all sorts of opportunities to share Jesus with them.

One spin-off of this idea is that smaller churches, especially in urban or suburban areas, can offer ESL courses to persons trying to learn English. There is no easier way to share the story of redemption with someone than by reading the Bible together. This is often exactly what happens when churches host ESL classes. Adults come to learn how to read and speak English and churches use the Bible as their primary textbook. Conversations about theological truths begin to occur naturally as the students are exposed night after night to God's inerrant word. There is a great need for ESL classes, especially if there is no charge to the students. ESL certification for the primary teacher of this ministry takes between six to twelve months and there is a moderate financial cost, but TESOL certification is not a requirement to teach ESL courses. It takes commitment, patience, and an attitude of service to labor together towards an achievable goal.

There are more options that could be listed here, and many more to be discovered as new challenges arise in a community. Look at your community, love the people around you, and seek to understand their needs. Don't let your size limit your willingness to do the most you can to reach your neighbors. But also, don't let your desire to help immediate needs limit the full scope of your mission.

In all of these actions, there is a temptation to provide a societal service (helping kids read better, provide financial assistance to keep a family in their home, etc.) but fail to tell them about Jesus. The gospel cannot fall to the wayside. Christianity has specifically called our mission

13. Fiester, *Early Warning*, 6.

"The Great Commission," as opposed to "A Pretty Good Suggestion." We are commanded to go into all the world and share the gospel that Jesus saves. To help a neighbor is good and right, but to withhold the gospel is sinful. Carl F. H. Henry once quipped, "The gospel is only good news if it gets there in time."[14]

Small churches can make a significant impact in their community—both from a social and a spiritual perspective—and around the globe, by partnering in global missions. In today's society, churches are no longer looked to for answers to moral questions. They are no longer seen as the foundation of societal stability or the fabric holding our nation together. Instead, they are being pushed to the margins and labeled as intolerant and sometimes hateful. But, as the old saying goes, actions speak louder than words. If churches intentionally invest in making their communities a better place, they transition from being the people who are against "fill-in-the-blank" to the people who are known for caring for their neighbors.

The early church was known for how they loved and cared for people. Regardless of congregation size, the mission is the same. We can reach our communities if we will only look outward. It may be the case that the church culture seems to acknowledge larger churches more than others. But our neighborhoods don't care about that—they are simply looking for hope in a broken world. Let us be known by our love, and let it be known that small churches are a great place to love others and be loved.

BIBLIOGRAPHY

Adopt Us Kids, "About the Children," https://www.adoptuskids.org/meet-the-children/children-in-foster-care/about-the-children.

Fiester, Leila. *Early Warning! Why Reading by the End of Third Grade Matters.* Baltimore: The Annie E. Casey Foundation, 2010. http://www.aecf.org/resources/early-warning-why-reading-by-the-end-of-third-grade-matters/#sthash.zyBGkKdx.dpbs.

"Foster Care Statistics 2015." https://www.childwelfare.gov/pubPDFs/foster.pdf#page=9&view=Race and ethnicity.

Hunter, James Davison. *To Change the World: The Irony, Tragedy, and Possibility of Christianity in the Late Modern World.* Oxford: Oxford University Press, 2010.

International Mission Board. "Key Terms." https://www.imb.org/beliefs-key-terms/#Unreached.

———. "Lesson 1: Unreached and Unengaged People Groups." https://www.imb.org/topic/explore-missions/missions-and-world-today/lesson-1-unreached-and-unengaged-people-groups.

14. Thornbury, *Recovering Classic Evangelicalism*, 175.

Lynn, Sheryl. "Francis Chan Goes Into Detail with Facebook Employees on Why He Left His Megachurch." *The Christian Post*. June 29, 2017. http://www.christianpost.com/news/francis-chan-goes-into-detail-with-facebook-employees-on-why-he-left-his-megachurch-190136

Payne, J. D. *Pressure Points: Twelve Global Issues Shaping the Face of the Church*. Nashville: Thomas Nelson, 2013.

Sills, David. *Changing World, Unchanging Mission: Responding to Global Challenges*. Downers Grove, IL: IVP, 2015.

Thornbury, Greg Allan. *Recovering Classic Evangelicalism: Applying the Wisdom and Vision of Carl F. H. Henry*. Wheaton, IL: Crossway, 2013.

http://public.imb.org/globalresearch/Pages/default.aspx.

2

Multiethnic Ministry in the Small Church

PAGE BROOKS

The radical and ethnic compositions of many communities in America have changed drastically over the past several decades. One can hardly go anywhere in America without encountering significant ethnic diversity. Can small churches, especially those with a part-time pastor or staff, embrace the diversity that often surrounds them?

I believe any church, empowered by the mission of the kingdom of God, can reach the diverse community that surrounds them. In fact, small churches with part-time staffs may have some advantages. In the following chapter, I will give a short personal testimony of how my wife and I came to desire multiethnic ministry (while we were serving in small churches), the biblical basis for diversity in church, strategies of how to embrace our multiethnic mission, and practical wisdom in ministries to diverse populations.

A BRIEF HISTORY OF CHURCH GROWTH IN THE LAST FEW DECADES

During the 1980s and 1990s, the church growth movement used the homogenous unit principle to sustain growth. C. Peter Wagner taught that demographically similar people can cause church growth the fastest.[1] Think about it: you can probably reach people with the gospel the quickest with people who are like you (education, race, socioeconomic background, etc.).

The principle of homogeneity fueled the church growth movement and produced some of the largest megachurches we have ever seen in the modern world. Most of these megachurches were in the suburbs of cities and were made up of people who liked the same style of worship, preaching, and ministry.

No doubt, the church growth movement has brought many people to follow Jesus. But, is it entirely biblical?

A LONGING TO SEE MORE COLOR

For many years my wife and I were involved in church plants and small churches that were just like us: white, middle-class, educated, and suburban. We planted churches with people that looked like us because that is what we were taught and it seemed the most logical way. After all, all my friends were like me and if I attracted more of them to my church, it would grow. Or, at least those were the principles I had believed.

In the early years of our marriage, my wife and I decided to adopt multiethnically. While the adoption stories of each of our three children are unique and filled with God's providential working hands, I will summarize by saying that God used our multiethnic adoptions to open our hearts to multiethnic church ministry.

At this point I need to share a little of my background to help the reader understand the dynamics of our family and setting. I was born in Montgomery, Alabama, and grew up in parts of Selma and Birmingham. I literally saw all the places where the Civil Rights struggle took place as I was reading about the events in my Alabama history book in school. My family had been through the Civil Rights events as well, seeing it all unfold in the cities in Alabama. Needless to say, multiethnic adoption was not an easy concept to work through for my family or myself.

Through these adoptions God opened our hearts to doing multiethnic churches. We started to realize that if our family was multiethnic, should

---

1. McGavran, *Understanding Church Growth*, 163. Peter Wagner has stated this principle in several church growth books. The very first time was in the first edition of *Understanding Church Growth*, when he stated, "People like to become Christians without crossing racial, linguistic, or class barriers."

not our church be as well? Before planting our first multiethnic church, God allowed us to be part of two successful, homogenous church plants. We are thankful for those churches and they are still ministering today by God's grace. However, we always felt like something was missing.

Anytime multiethnic ministry is done in churches, it is usually done in ways that might not be helpful. For example, a church may decide to do ministry in a certain area of town. They may do a block party, or take food to certain families. Often these families are of a different race or ethnicity than the church. While the ministry may have good motivations, there is no real integration of the people into the church. There is always a mentality of "us" ministering to "them."

Circumstances like these, and more, eventually led us to do multiethnic church planting. One time I was speaking at a church on multiethnic ministry and one lady perhaps had the best reason of all to do multiethnic churches. She said, "I live in a multiethnic world, and work in a multiethnic place. Why can't I worship in a multiethnic church?" Exactly! With the world around us changing and becoming more multiethnic, our churches need to embrace the change that is coming and plant multiethnic churches to reach a multiethnic world.

THE CHANGING PICTURE OF FACES IN AMERICA

Why should our churches be multiethnic? There are some practical reasons that multiethnic churches need to exist in America.

First, we are experiencing an increase in immigration in the United States. From cities to rural areas, immigration is having a huge influence. Cities become exposed to immigrants and refugees as they settle due to governmental relocation programs, family, or job opportunities. Immigrants also exist in large populations in rural areas, often around farming communities. There is almost no place in the United States that a person cannot go without seeing the effects of the presence of immigrants.

Second, urbanization is also creating cities that are multiethnic. In the next decade or two, there will be more people living in cities than in rural areas for the first time in history. Urbanization has created cities that are no longer monoethnic, but are attracting people from all around the world. The affect is not only in larger cities, but now in smaller towns as well. The urbanization creates opportunities for churches that can literally reach the world within their own city.

Third, the denominations in the United States have a long history of systemic racism. By systemic racism I mean many of our denominations were formed because of the separation of the races in the earliest history of the United States. Often whites worshipped separately from black slaves. If they did worship together, the slaves were often seated separately. Several new denominations were formed due to these separations. For example, the African Methodist Episcopal church (and its forerunners) was founded because blacks worshipped separately from whites in the early Protestant Episcopal Church.

Today, whether intentionally or not, denominations continue the separation. Yes, worship styles and preferences have now developed over the decades and even centuries. But, an opportunity now exists in our society to correct the racism that developed at the founding of the United States. With the increase in immigration, travel to and from other countries, and technology that unites the world, churches have an opportunity like never before to truly be a local manifestation of the heavenly vision from Revelation for all the ethnicities of the world to worship together in a local church.

IS IT BIBLICAL?

I propose that God intended his covenant people (Old Testament) and the church (New Testament) to be multiethnic from the beginning. The gospel, if proclaimed correctly by his people and church, should produce a people who are representative of every nation, tribe, and tongue. But the question is how does that happen exactly, and what does it look like?

The first passage people often reference concerning the multiethnic vision of the church is Revelation 7:9: "After this I looked, and there before me was a great multitude that no one could count, from every nation, tribe, people and language, standing before the throne and before the Lamb. They were wearing white robes and were holding palm branches in their hands" (NIV).

We know in the end God will bring all people together so that heaven will be multiethnic, but since the beginning of the Bible we see where God intended for his covenant people to be multiethnic. When God was making his promise to Abram to make him the father of many nations (ethnicities), God used what might be considered multiethnic wording: "all the families of the earth will be blessed . . . ;" and "in your seed all the nations of the earth will be blessed" (ESV). From the start, God was laying the foundation for his people to be from all the various ethnicities of the world.

Other passages from the Old Testament speak to the multiethnicity that God desires for his people. The people of Israel were, from the start, supposed to be a witness to the peoples around them. The book of Jonah is about getting the message of God to people other than the covenant people of Israel. Isaiah 46:6 speaks of how God will make the nation of Israel and the Messiah a light to the nations (Gentiles) so his message goes to the ends of the earth.

In the New Testament, the multiethnic theme becomes even more pronounced. Jesus often crossed over traditional ethnic and cultural boundaries. The story of Jesus' encounter with the Samaritan woman shows that Jesus' mission was to reach out to not only the Jews, but also their enemies.

The book of Acts displays how the church specifically carries out its multiethnic mission. Acts 10:9–16: "'Surely not, Lord!' Peter replied. 'I have never eaten anything impure or unclean.' The voice spoke to him a second time, 'Do not call anything impure that God has made clean.' This happened three times, and immediately the sheet was taken back to heaven." Often this passage is interpreted along two primary themes. First, that the Old Testament law has passed and now everything can be considered clean before the Lord. Second, that the gospel is not just for the Jews, but for non-Jews (Gentiles) as well. While all the above is true, I also want to call attention to the fact that there are multicultural themes also present in this passage. Later in the chapter, Peter stands and proclaims that the gospel is not just for the Jews, but for the Gentiles, whom he considered unclean. They were considered unclean in Peter's mind, not just because of the law, but because of their ethnicity. Notice in verse 10:34, he uses the language of ethnicity ("every nation") to show that any person who fears God can now believe in Jesus Christ for salvation.

Think about it, here is Peter, probably ten years or more after Pentecost, and still he is only proclaiming the gospel to the Jews. It took a vision from God to show him that the gospel is meant to transcend not just religious lines (i.e., the Law), but ethnic and racial lines as well. I believe this passage shows us that the early church had ethnic and racial church issues, in a similar way in which we do today.

We could cover many passages in the New Testament that speak to a multicultural theme. The formation of the office of deacon was not only to take the weight of ministry off the apostles, but it was over an ethnicity issue (Greek widows not being served). Paul writes in Romans about how the gospel is now for the Gentiles. Further, Paul writes in Galatians about how the gospel is for any person, regardless of gender, background, or ethnicity (Gal 3:28).

It should be clear by now that the gospel is meant to produce a saved people that represent a multicultural church. This is the way God intended it from the beginning, even in the early church! This study also shows us that ethnicity and race were major hindrances in the early church.

One final point needs to be made concerning the multiethnic church in the New Testament. The most basic definition of the gospel is that anyone who believes upon Jesus Christ and his good news can be saved. However, I believe the New Testament clearly shows that one of the first-order implications of the gospel is it should produce a church that is multicultural. Yet humans, by our very nature, produce hindrances to the furtherance of the gospel. The New Testament clearly shows that ethnicity was one of the first hindrances to the spread of the gospel and had to be overcome immediately.

Ethnicity—and by extension, race—is a primary hindrance to the gospel because our churches are still separated along the lines of ethnicity and race. The power of the gospel saves, but it should also produce a church that reflects the multiethnicity that God has desired from the Day of Pentecost!

STEPS TO BECOME A MULTIETHNIC CHURCH

Know the Demographics of Your Community

If we truly see our communities as a mission field, then one of the primary goals of every local church should be to reflect their community. Often times, however, churches do not look like their communities. Even if a community is highly monoethnic, there will certainly be socioeconomic, educational, generational, and other differences that a congregation should reflect. This is why one of the first steps toward a church becoming multiethnic is for the church to understand their community.

Today there is a preponderance of demographic data that is easily available to local churches. Sources of this data may include local organizations, the newspaper, websites, and denominational offices. It is important for a church first to determine their general reach in a geographic area. For example a church may have people who drive only two or three miles to church if they are in a dense urban area. However, rural churches may draw from several miles away. If a church is located near an interstate they may also draw people from several miles away.

Once a church determines their reach, they can find demographic data for that particular area. The church leadership should ensure they are familiar with the area by walking or driving around in order to expose themselves to the various groups found in their demographic data. I am personally amazed at how many times pastors who have lived in areas for years still do not know what demographics of people live in the backyard of their own churches.

Pastors then need to compare the makeup of their own church to what they find in their communities. For example if a community is predominantly white or black, their churches may very well be predominantly white or black. However their community may be 80 percent white, 10 percent black, and 10 percent Asian. The pastor should ask if his congregation represents and reflects the demographic percentages in the community.

One of the myths of the multicultural church movement is that a church has to be made up of different colors of skin in order to truly be a multiethnic church. However if a community is predominantly white or black, and a church in that location is predominantly white or black, then that is great! The church does not necessarily have to go out and find people of another skin color just to say that they are multiethnic or multicultural. Even within races, diversity can exist.

For example, does the church represent the socioeconomic and educational diversity that is in a particular area? If a church is made up of all rich or all middle-class people, and there is a great deal of socioeconomic diversity in their local area, then the church needs to ask themselves if they are truly reaching their community.

Pastors and church leadership should also consider growing trends of diversity. With immigration patterns, it is not uncommon for communities to be experiencing growth in particular ethnicities. In some cities, Hispanic and Asian populations are increasing. The church should notice such trends and ask themselves how they can make plans in the future to reach a growing demographic group.

The primary point is that a church should reflect the demographics they have in their area of reach. Too often churches consist of only one demographic group while their communities are quite diverse. Or a community has changed, and the church has stayed the same over the years. The first step of the strategy in being a multiethnic church is simply knowing who is in your community and if the church is indeed reaching them.

When is a church truly considered to be multiethnic? A great deal of debate exists on the exact numbers, but normally if a church is no more than between 70 percent to 80 percent of one ethnicity, then the church is considered to be multiethnic.[2]

Forming a Multiethnic Core Leadership

An important step in creating a multiethnic church is having a multi-ethnic core leadership. By core leadership, I am including pastors, staff, leadership positions, and core membership. If we want our churches to reflect the diversity of our communities, then it follows that we must have multiethnic leadership.

Why should a church consider people of various ethnicities to be part of the leadership? First, the goal of a multiethnic church is to reflect the diversity that God desires in heaven. There is the practical reality that people of common background can often reach people like them better than others (the homogeneous unit principle). For example, educated persons often associate more with other educated persons. Business people tend to be friends with other business people. What circle of friends do you personally have? If you are white, most likely your friends are white. If you are black, most likely your friends are black. We tend to be able to share the gospel with those who are most like us.

Second, to reach certain populations, specific skills may be needed. A Hispanic pastor will be able to relate linguistically and culturally to other Hispanics. A church may need to hire such staff members to specifically relate to those target populations in a community. For example, a majority white church may want to hire a Hispanic pastor if they have a Hispanic population. Similarly, a majority black church may want to hire a white pastor if they desire to reach a growing white population in their community.

Third, a church can communicate to the community how serious they are about being a diverse community by having diversity in their leadership. It shows the community that a church values the contributions of other ethnicities to the ministries of the church. Hispanics generally have closer family and community relationships. African-Americans sometimes

---

2. Sociologist Michael Emerson makes a persuasive case for the 80% rule. Emerson and Woo, *People of the Dream*, 35.

have livelier worship. We all can learn from each other when we share in the fellowship of the church together rather than apart.

If a church is new (like a church plant), then the church needs to be intentional about having diversity in its leadership. Church plants may find it easier to instill such values from the start. Many church plants begin with the pastoral team being diverse as the diversity in pastoral leadership communicates that a church is strongly committed to reaching a diverse community. A church plant should also recruit diverse people into its core team. One church plant in Kentucky purposefully asked both white and black families to join their core team because they wanted to represent the diversity of the city. That diversity has continued to expand as the church has grown.

Allow me to give a brief word on how the homogeneous unit principle relates to the multiethnic church. Yes, the homogeneous unit principle is very useful in reaching people. The difference is that in a multiethnic church, monoethnic relationships are brought together to form a multiethnic fellowship as people are reached with the gospel. This was, in fact, the original intention of Donald McGavran![3]

A careful balance must be kept as the building of diversity is emphasized while at the same time reaching people who are alike. Jesus taught us that whatever our life situation, we are to reach those who are around us and like us. At the same time, he also taught us that we should be willing to step out of our normal circumstances to relate to those who are different from us. While our personal relationships may vary, the local church should reflect the overall diversity in a community as a reflection of heaven. Yes, a Hispanic congregation may meet in the same building as a white congregation and have separate services primarily because of linguistic differences, but the two congregations should do all they can to show their unity in Christ.

Let me say a word about recruiting leadership based upon diversity. Never should a church recruit a member of the staff, leadership, or core team based simply upon race or ethnicity. Biblical qualifications should exist for church members, core leaders, and pastors, and no person should be exempt simply because of race or ethnicity. Sometimes, however, churches

---

3. Donald McGavran is the father of the Church Growth Movement. He proposed the Homogeneous Unit Principle as a key factor in church growth. A full explanation can be found in the Lausanne Occasional Paper, "The Pasadena Consultation: Homogeneous Unit Principle, 1978." This paper can be found at https://www.lausanne.org/content/lop/lop-1.

or church plants do not pray enough for, or put the energy into finding, qualified leaders from diverse backgrounds.

To start the process of diversifying a church, a church must start with the most visible leadership of the church. This shows the church is not merely talking about diversity, but also doing something about it. The process may be slow, but as the church embraces and shows its commitment to biblical diversity and reaching the diverse population of their community, the message will be clearly observed in word and action.

FIVE-FOLD TEST

A growing, multiethnic church should always keep a balance between the pursuit of diversity and the pursuit of making disciples. Pursuing multiethnicity should be a natural part of the disciple-making process. The gospel compels us to go make disciples of all nations, so the gospel should naturally lead to a multiethnic community. However, some multiethnic churches become so driven by the pursuit of multiethnicity that they forget about making disciples.

In the early years of our church plant, we always walked a tight-rope between disciple-making and multiethnicity. We started the church with a multiethnic vision, so I was driven to ensure that our people reflected that multiethnic focus. Discipleship was always a part of our DNA, but it was often hard to keep a balance between the two. A few years into the church plant, we faced a significant shift. Several of our multiethnic leadership left, both whites and African-Americans. Some felt we were not doing enough to diversify, and others thought we were doing too much! After the dust settled, our leadership was all the more determined to ensure we kept a balance between the two. We knew we would never do anything perfectly, but by relying upon the Spirit, we would attempt it.

From that experience came a five-fold test we developed for our local congregation. This test originated with the Evangelical Covenant Church and is used by several denominations. We use it as a guideline for ensuring that every ministry initiative promotes diversity. We took the test and transformed it for our purposes at the local church level. Every ministry initiative we started was filtered through the test to help us keep the balance between discipleship and diversity. Discipleship was always our primary mission; discipleship of the various ethnicities represented in our community was our target. The test helped us to diversify our ministries and outreach to fit our target.

Here is the five-fold test we developed:

> Canal Street Church: A Mosaic Community seeks to fulfill our vision of seeing life-transformation among all people by having a diverse community of Christ-followers. Our mission is to make disciples of all peoples and ethnicities. We specifically envision a church that is diverse in race, ethnicity, and economic status in a city that is deeply divided by such factors. To that end, we have developed the following questions to act as a framework for guiding us in every ministry of our church to ensure we are reaching our diverse community and city.
>
> 1. Population: Are we identifying, reaching, and embracing increasing numbers of people among diverse racial and ethnic populations in our local community? What groups do we need to reach specifically?
>
> 2. Participation: How intentionally are we looking for ways to engage life together? What biases are currently embedded in our values and operation that keep us from participating together?
>
> 3. Power: Are the positions and structures of leadership in our church's ministries influenced by the perspectives and gifts of diverse racial and ethnic populations? Are we actively seeking to disciple and raise up leadership among our diverse members?
>
> 4. Pace-Setting: Having been informed by the additional perspectives, burdens, and gifts that our racial and ethnic diversity brings to us, what new mission opportunities is the church now better positioned to strengthen and initiate? What are the cultural considerations of each ministry initiative that help us reach our diverse community?
>
> 5. Purposeful Narrative: How do the stories of people from new backgrounds become incorporated into the church's history as we seek to truly understand our brothers and sisters from diverse backgrounds? How do all of these streams flow together into one story, moving forward together to reach others for Christ?[4]

Allow me to give two practical examples of how we applied the test. First, we used the questions to assess our greeting ministry. If we truly wanted to reflect the community both on the outside of the church, as well as on the inside of the church, then we needed to diversify our greeters. The majority of our greeters were white. While we appreciated their service and

---

4. More information about the Five-Fold Test can be found at: http://www.covchurch.org/wp-content/uploads/sites/2/2011/02/2-Five-fold-Test.pdf

volunteerism, we wanted to make sure that whoever came to our church from the community truly felt welcome by seeing people like themselves at our front doors. This was merely a small step toward connecting with people for the ultimate purpose of discipleship.

Second, we assessed our community groups. While our groups were fairly diverse, the majority of our community group leaders were white. The five-fold test challenged us to raise up and train leaders from various ethnicities to ensure we were continually reaching diverse populations of people at the small-group level.

It is helpful for each church to develop guidelines such as these to help the church maintain their primary focus on evangelism and discipleship, and not just diversity.

Worship Considerations

Worship can be an opportunity and challenge for the multicultural church. Worship preferences go down to the core of who we are and no doubt there have been many church struggles over worship preferences. For the multiethnic church perspective, however, these differences need to be seen as something of beauty. In other words, even though God created many different people of races and ethnicities with different skin and eye colors, when they are seen together they are quite beautiful. In the same way, when we bring together the various styles of worship, they can be seen as expressions of beauty in the way that we as believers respond to God.

The various worship styles in a multicultural church can be seen as an opportunity to learn and express ourselves in ways that perhaps we have not considered before. Generally, white churches tend to be more quiet and reverent. African-American churches tend to be livelier and more celebratory. The Spanish churches tend to be more spirit-filled. White preachers tend to be more intellectual. Black preachers tend to be more animated. While these are generalizations and stereotypes, my point is to show that there are wonderful riches in the backgrounds of these various types of churches from which we can borrow. No church has worship completely figured out.

In a multicultural church, worship is seen as an opportunity for people from various backgrounds to express themselves in various fashions. It is also an opportunity for those from other cultures and backgrounds to learn to express themselves in other ways. But if we are truly to reflect the fact that in heaven different languages and tongues will be spoken giving praise to God, we should go ahead and get used to that in our worship here on earth!

What are some ways multicultural churches can transform their worship to reflect the people of their community? First, church should look at the people in their community and ask what style of worship reflects that population best. This is an issue wherein many churches will have to decide they are willing to change their style of worship to reflect the community. For example, a majority white church may need to decide to incorporate styles of African-American church worship into their service. Or a church may decide to start incorporating Hispanic songs with Spanish lyrics into their worship.

Third, a church should look for a leader who is able to bring about the changes and incorporate the diversity into the worship. The worship leader does not necessarily have to be fluent in other styles of worship per se. I believe the primary consideration for worship leaders is that they are willing to incorporate people with various gifts and from various music styles into the worship team. No one worship leader or musician can fulfill all the varying styles that may be represented in a multiethnic church. Instead, the worship leader should be a facilitator of others whom God may send to the church to help lead the worship.

Finally, churches should look for ways to include people in the other aspects of worship, such as prayers, Scripture readings, announcements, and other parts of the service. The people who perform these parts of the service should reflect the diversity that is in the congregation. In my own church, we will have an African-American, Hispanic, a man, a woman, an older adult, and a young child all help leading the same worship service.

Opportunities with Baptism and the Communion

Multiethnic churches should be encouraged to practice the ordinances of the church very often.

While baptism and Communion (or the Lord's Supper) are practiced at different times in the spiritual life of the church, they can be seen as opportunities to show unity in diversity. Baptism is only conducted once in the life of the person when the person comes into the covenant community of God. It symbolizes new life and is an outward expression of an inward reality. Communion is practiced often, and in some traditions every Sunday.

Baptism services can be seen as a time to encourage that the diversity of the church be shown. Depending upon the denominational tradition, one of the ministers or a layperson may administer the baptism. If a pastor or layperson is leading the baptism, it is a wonderful time to have the various ethnicities represented, especially if a cross-cultural discipling relationship developed between the two persons.

Communion is perhaps an even greater way of showing the unity in diversity of the church. The symbolism of Communion has horizontal and vertical implications. The vertical implication is, of course, our sharing in the bread and cup of Christ at the time of Communion. We participate and fellowship with Christ in a spiritual manner as we take the elements of the Supper (1 Cor 10:16). Our unity comes as we gather together around the bread and the cup because of our oneness in Jesus Christ that is symbolized around the table.

The horizontal relationship is given in the symbolism of the members of the church family coming around the common table. Believers from various backgrounds come together to participate in the Supper and in doing so, commune together based upon their unity with Christ. Even more importantly, Paul commanded believers in 1 Corinthians 11:28 to make sure their relationships were right with one another before coming before the table. Often this verse is used to speak of how believers should examine themselves concerning their relationship with the Lord before taking Communion, but actually Paul commands the believer to examine himself or herself in relation to other believers. I believe this shows that our horizontal relationships are just as important as our vertical relationship, though the former is always based upon the latter.

At our church we intentionally try to show the diversity in our body when we celebrate Communion, which we do every Sunday. I regularly have our assistant pastors share in the celebration of Communion, especially if I am leading other parts of worship. We also have laypeople serving the elements, and deliberately have persons from different ethnicities represented as they serve. The visual is quite stunning.

Allow me to say a few words of caution and perhaps answer a few questions. Never should the ordinances be done merely to put on a show for the sake of diversity. Baptism and Communion are sacred acts and should only be celebrated on the proper occasions. When they are celebrated at the proper occasions, it can be a joyous time of worship. In the same way, those helping in the celebration of baptism and Communion should be properly trained and held accountable in what they do. Never should a person be thrust in front of people merely to put on a show of diversity. For example, every person we allow to serve the Lord's Supper is a leader in our church in some way and has been trained in what to do.

Using Other Resources to Reach Diverse Populations

A church may be able to use its people and material resources in other ways to reach the diverse populations in their community.

The church building itself can be a great resource. If a church is small and supports a part-time pastor, the church may not be used a great deal during the week. The church may choose to open its building to allow specific groups to meet or worship there. An ethnic group might need space to conduct a native-language worship service, but they may be too small to afford their own building. The church may open its building to such a group for them to be able to worship at an affordable rent. For example, a church in Northeast Atlanta at one time had eight different native-language churches hosted in its building!

Immigrant and refugee populations are increasing across the world, and there are many opportunities in the United States for ministry to these groups. Churches may partner with local non-profit groups to help immigrant and refugee families that live in the area. Families are often in need of people to simply come along beside them to help find jobs, setup their homes, and enroll children in schools. Churches may also decide to host groups that provide low or no-cost help to these populations, such as legal advice.

ESL classes have become a very popular way to help. Most immigrants and refugees have a desire to learn English as they incorporate into society. My church has hosted an ESL class for years to the Hispanic population in our area of the city, and has found it to be a wonderful gateway of ministry to Hispanic families.

Churches may also decide to partner with other churches for special occasions, simply to show the community that there is unity among churches. I know many white and black churches that have conducted joint worship services during Easter or Christmas to show unity. Or, different churches have come together to perform an outreach of some kind in a community, such as a block party. Churches coming together, even for brief periods of time, can have a powerful witness to the community.

The above ministries are only examples of some of the more popular ways to reach out to diverse populations in the community. Churches can use such ministries to begin their journey toward being a multiethnic church. Allow me to give a word of encouragement and a word of caution. While it may be encouraging for a church to do ministry to a certain population in their community, such an outreach does not necessarily make them a multiethnic church. It may be a good first step, but I believe God wants us to do even more to show the unity of his kingdom!

A FINAL ENCOURAGEMENT

The road to becoming a multiethnic church can be long and arduous. It requires purposeful decisions, a prayerful spirit, and watchful patience. For a church with a part-time pastor, the DNA of multiethnicity can be laid from the beginning. For an established church with a part-time pastor, the process may take years. Nevertheless, I believe the process is worth the effort because of the clear Gospel calling we have as churches to reach all ethnicities with the love of Jesus Christ.

BIBLIOGRAPHY

DeYmaz, Mark. *Building a Healthy Multi-Ethnic Church: Mandate, Commitments, and Practices of a Diverse Congregation*. San Francisco: Leadership Network Publications, 2007.

Emerson, Michael O. *Divided by Faith: Evangelical Religion and the Problem of Race in America*. New York: Oxford University Press, 2000.

Emerson, Michael O., and Rodney M. Woo. *People of the Dream: Multiracial Congregations in the United States*. Princeton: Princeton University Press, 2006.

The Evangelical Covenant Church. "Session Two: The Five-fold Test." http://www.covchurch.org/wp-content/uploads/sites/2/2011/02/2-Five-fold-Test.pdf.

McGavran, Donald. *Understanding Church Growth*. 3rd ed. Revised and edited by C. Peter Wagner. Grand Rapids: Eerdmans, 1990.

McGavran, Donald, and Wayne Weld. *Principles of Church Growth*. South Pasadena, CA: William Carey Library, 1974.

Woo, Rodney. *The Color of Church*. Nashville: B and H Academic, 2009.

SECTION 2

Small-Church Pastoral Ministry

3

Evangelism in the Small Church

JAKE ROUDKOVSKI

For the past three decades, it has been my distinct privilege to minister as pastor of several small churches that experienced spiritual as well as numerical growth. In addition to my role as a professor at New Orleans Baptist Theological Seminary, I currently serve as a bivocational pastor of a small church. Challenges associated with leading a small church in evangelism are many, ranging from limited staff and resources to at times spiritually lethargic membership and unfavorable demographics. In spite of the challenges, the small church holds amazing potential for reaching people with the gospel of Christ.

In this chapter, an attempt will be made to delineate seven principles to undergird evangelistic efforts in the small church. The list of principles will not be comprehensive, but rather providing a starting point for pastors desirous to reach people for Christ in their communities. Experienced veterans of pastoral ministry may find these principles useful in reinforcing intentionality and accountability for evangelism in the small church.

EVANGELISM IS NOT OPTIONAL

First of all, church leaders must be willing to embrace a biblical reality that evangelism is not optional. It may be helpful at this point to define the word evangelism. Evangelism comes from the Greek verb ευαγγελιζo (*euangelizo*) meaning "to announce, proclaim, or bring good news." The verb form is found thirty-three times in the New Testament. The noun form ευαγγελιον (*euangelion*) meaning "gospel, good news, or evangel" is found seventy-six times in the New Testament. Evangelism is sharing the good news.

Jesus began his proclamation ministry by sharing the good news in Mark 1:14–15 calling people to "believe in the gospel." Later in Mark 1:17, Jesus called Simon and Andrew to follow him, promising he would make them "fishers of men." Christ exemplified what it meant to be "fishers of men" by sharing the good news. Leighton Ford highlighted thirty-five evangelistic encounters of Jesus in the Gospels.[1] Allow me to give some examples. In John 3, Jesus engaged in evangelistic encounter with Nicodemus. In John 4, Christ witnessed to the Samaritan woman, who came to believe in Christ. In John 18, Jesus testified to Pilate who rejected his witness. In addition to embodying what it means to be "fishers of men," Christ provided training opportunities for his followers to share the good news. In Luke 10:1–12, Christ sent seventy of his followers to engage people with the gospel. In the same context, Jesus encouraged his disciples to pray for more harvest workers implying that the workers of the kingdom were those who shared the good news. Before his ascension, Christ issued the Great Commission that demanded sharing of the good news (Matt 28:18–20; Mark 16:15; Luke 24:46–49; John 20:21; Acts 1:8). Paul later defined the good news as the death, burial, and resurrection of Jesus Christ (1 Cor 15:1–5).

The book of Acts unfolded as the followers of Christ engaged the world with the good news. On the day of Pentecost described in Acts 2, Peter preached a Holy Spirit-empowered evangelistic message that resulted in 3,000 new believers. The powerful proclamation of the gospel by Peter was preceded by 120 followers of Christ sharing the good news on the Day of Pentecost. As Roy Fish, a legendary professor of evangelism, pointed out, "If the private witnessing had not preceded Peter's sermon, there was the least likelihood that any such results would have followed."[2] The book of Acts is replete with examples of how not only Peter but the apostles and their close associates engaged in sharing the good news. Philip communicated his faith successfully to an Ethiopian eunuch in Acts 8. Peter reluctantly, but effectively, witnessed to Cornelius in Acts 10. Paul led Roman proconsul Sergius Paulus to faith in Christ in Acts 13.

1. Ford, *The Christian Persuader*, 67.
2. Fish, *Every Member Evangelism for Today*, 11.

The believers who came to faith in Christ as the result of the evangelistic ministry of the apostles and their close associates caught Christ's vision for sharing the good news. In Acts 8:4, believers, who were forced out of Jerusalem by persecution, began to proclaim the gospel wherever they went. In Acts 11:19, the rank-and-file believers were sharing their faith with Jews in Antioch. In Acts 11:20, men of Cyrene and Cyprus were sharing the good news with the Gentiles in the same city. The early church in Antioch was birthed as a result of faithful sharing of the gospel.

From a limited examination of New Testament evangelistic narratives, a compelling picture emerges in which sharing the good news was a central part of the ministry of Jesus and the early church. Jesus proclaimed the good news, trained his disciples to share the good news, and commanded his followers to share the good news. The early church obeyed his command as they engaged the world with the good news. Evangelism was not optional for Christ, his disciples, or the early church, and it is not optional for the contemporary church.

PRAYER IS FOUNDATIONAL

Secondly, prayer is a foundational ingredient for effective evangelism in the small church. The pastor should lead his congregation to pray by name for the lost people. It has been my practice to list the names of lost people in my journal and blank pages in the front and the back of my Bible. As God allows the individuals to come to faith in Christ, I place the date that God answered my prayer in regard to their salvation. As the pastor prays for the lost people by name, it gives him moral and spiritual authority to encourage his people to do the same. Recently, I began using the ministry of Bless Every Home.[3] The free website makes available a list of people in a selected neighborhood to pray by name. Subscribers regularly receive an email with names of people to pray for and even a sample prayer. In leading church members to embrace their responsibility to pray for the salvation of their neighbors, the ministry of Bless Every Home serves as a helpful tool.

Since contemporary pastors live in a visual society, it may be beneficial to find creative ways to illustrate visually people's commitment to pray evangelistically. During a renovation process in one church, we had a number of available bricks from the old building. Church members were asked to pray for the lost by name during the year. As a token of their commitment, they

---

3. www.blesseveryhome.com

were to inscribe on a brick the first name of a person they were committing to pray. Every time they came to church, their brick or bricks provided a visual reminder to pray for the lost. When the person being prayed for came to know Christ, the brick with his or her name was placed on the other side of the church building designated as The Victory Wall. It was fascinating and encouraging to observe the growth of The Victory Wall constructed from the bricks with names of people coming to Christ.

Another church erected a wooden cross placed at the front of their auditorium. Several weeks before Easter, the pastor challenged his people to commit to pray evangelistically by nailing a list with the names of the lost to the cross. As church members prayed for the names of the lost, they were to share a verbal witness with them. When a verbal witness was attempted, the church members were asked to place a green rope on a nail holding his or her list. If a person came to faith in Christ, a red rope was used. As the weeks progressed toward Easter, most of the nails were filled with ropes signifying a verbal witness to the lost person with several ropes symbolizing the acceptance of Christ. The church experienced the largest Easter attendance in their history with many people trusting Christ as their Savior and Lord.

As pastors lead their churches to pray for the lost, they must consider development of a strong prayer ministry team. In my first church, we challenged our people to become a part of the prayer ministry. Several who responded were equipped in prayer practices. They became the core of the prayer ministry team. They came to the church facility on a weekly basis and prayed for different prayer needs including the lost. The small church grew exponentially as the attempt was made to saturate every aspect and endeavor of the church with prayer.

In my current church, every Wednesday night we have a list of the lost people that church members pray for by name. In addition, anyone can send a name of a lost person to our prayer chain coordinator who, in turn, texts the prayer request to the members of the prayer ministry team. Every week, the prayer ministry team receives a number of requests to pray for lost relatives, friends, co-workers, and neighbors. When a person comes to faith in Christ, he or she is added to the prayer list and is kept there for a year as the church lifts him or her in prayer regularly. When I was a seminary student, I was asked to give Roy Fish a ride to the airport. During the ride, I asked the renowned professor, "Dr. Fish, if the church were to do just one thing to help recently converted believers, what would it be?" He responded without hesitation, "Praying for them by name!"

Without consistent prayer for the lost, the small church will not be able to reach its evangelistic potential. Charles Spurgeon defined the church's goal in regard to prayer in the following way:

> "If sinners will be damned, at least let them leap to hell over our bodies. And if they will perish, let them perish with our arms about their knees, imploring them to stay. If hell must be filled, at least let it be filled in the teeth of our exertions, and let not one go there unwarned and unprayed for."[4]

The goal of any church is that every person in their circle and sphere of influence is prayed for in regard to his or her salvation.

RELY ON THE HOLY SPIRIT

The third principle for evangelism in the small church is the absolute necessity to rely upon the Holy Spirit. The Holy Spirit is the third person of Triune God who is indispensable to the task of evangelism. Without the Holy Spirit, a lost person cannot come to faith in Christ since it is the Holy Spirit who brings conviction (John 16:8) and a new birth (John 3:1–6). It is not the role of a believer to bring conviction to the lost; the role is reserved for the Holy Spirit. Recently at a local church, several individuals professed Christ publicly after the message. An individual came to me and said, "Pastor, thank you for saving those souls!" I had to explain to the person that I could not save anyone, it is God who saves by bringing conviction and new birth through the Holy Spirit. The responsibility of the soul-winner is not to convict an individual or even to bring him or her to a point of decision; it is the role of the Holy Spirit. The responsibility of the pastor and church members is to faithfully share the good news.

The pastor and church members will be freed from fears and anxieties when they realize that the Holy Spirit is at work in the lives of all lost people (John 16:7–10). Before the believer speaks to the unbeliever about Jesus, the Holy Spirit has already been working in the life of the unbeliever. The Holy Spirit may have spoken to that person through a general revelation of God, through nature, and/or a passage of Scripture. The Holy Spirit may have placed other people who witnessed to the unbeliever, and/or the Holy Spirit

4. Spurgeon, *Spurgeon at His Best*, 67.

may have created circumstances which allowed that person to be more sensitive to spiritual realities. A helpful tool in illustrating the aforementioned concept is the Spider Principle.[5] The work of the Holy Spirit is to create a web; drawing people to salvation. The Holy Spirit connects our message to that of other believers, circumstances, general revelation through nature, and specific revelation through the word of God. When the believer shares the good news of Christ with the unbeliever, he or she is adding another strand to the web that the Holy Spirit of God has been working on to draw the unbeliever to faith in Christ.

Since the Holy Spirit is indispensable to the task of evangelism, the pastor should rely upon the Holy Spirit in his witnessing encounters. The pastor has a responsibility to educate his church members about the role of the Holy Spirit and to emphasize the absolute necessity of relying upon the Holy Spirit in evangelism.

PASTOR'S EXAMPLE

Fourthly, the pastor must lead in evangelism. Paul encouraged Timothy to do "the work of an evangelist" (2 Tim 4:5). In my doctoral dissertation involving research of 314 pastors, the practice of personal evangelism was the strongest predictor for evangelistic growth of the church as evidenced by baptisms.[6] Even though teaching church members how to witness and preaching messages that encouraged church members to be intentionally evangelistic were correlated with more baptisms, it was what the pastor did in the area of personal evangelism that seemed to have a greater impact upon evangelistic effectiveness of the church. The practice of personal evangelism provided credibility to pastoral efforts in equipping church members in personal evangelism skills.

At our seminary, students and faculty members are encouraged to embrace the Caskey Challenge to witness to at least one lost person per week. It is a worthy goal for any church leader! When the pastor shares Christ with others, he may want to incorporate some of his experiences into his sermons. When the pastor shares how he may have overcome his fears and relied on the Holy Spirit for witnessing, his transparency and authenticity provide inspiration and motivation for church members to be

5. Kelley, *Adult Roman Road Witnessing Training Teacher's Guide*, 8.

6. Roudkovski, "An Investigation into a Relationship between Pastoral Personal Evangelism and Baptisms in Selected Southern Baptist Churches."

intentional about sharing the good news with others. As a seminary student I heard Gray Allison, a famed evangelism professor, say in class, "We never fail in witnessing, we only fail when we don't witness." Such a reminder will be liberating to any church member serious about personal evangelism.

As the pastor leads his people in personal evangelism, he should consider teaching a witnessing class periodically. Such resources as *One-On-One: Evangelism Made Simple* and *3 Circles Evangelism Kit*[7] may help the pastor train his church members to share the good news. In providing a class for witnessing, the pastor and church leaders may need to consider providing hands-on opportunities for class participants to share Christ with the lost.

INTENTIONALLY REACHING CHILDREN AND YOUTH

The fifth principle for evangelism in the small church involves intentionality in reaching children and youth. Since around 80 percent of people come to know Christ before they turn twenty,[8] the small church must be willing to prioritize reaching this receptive audience. It is beyond the scope of the chapter to have a comprehensive discussion on the age and the stage of accountability.[9] It is my personal conviction that when a child enters the stage of moral awareness he or she can come to faith in Christ.

Several New Testament passages have informed this conviction. From 2 Timothy 3:15, the implication can be made that Timothy followed Christ from childhood. Jesus said, "Let the little children come to me, and do not forbid them; for such is the kingdom of God" (Mark 10:14). In Matthew 18:6, Jesus warned those who "causes one of these little ones who believe in me to stumble," (NASB). The word Jesus employs for "believe" in the verse is the same one used in John 3:16, Acts 16:31, and Romans 10:9–10. According to Christ, children can believe in Christ.

Church leaders will do well to heed the encouragement of Charles Spurgeon, the prince of preachers, "Let none despise the stirrings of the Spirit in the hearts of the young. Let not boyish anxieties and juvenile repentances be lightly regarded. I, at least, can bear my personal testimony to the fact that grace operates on some minds at a period almost too early for

---

7. Information regarding these evangelism resources is available in the bibliography.

8. Rainer, *The Bridger Generation*, 14.

9. For a more detailed discussion on the topic, see Reid, *Evangelism Handbook*, 411–16.

recollection."[10] The pastor who does not want to disregard the work of the Holy Spirit in the lives of children should be willing to lead his church to invest time and efforts in reaching children and youth.

Several practical actions may be helpful in enabling the small church to be more intentional in reaching children and youth. The pastor may want to equip parents in the church to reach their children for Christ. Even though Christian parents tend to bring their children to their pastor for conversion conversations, the pastor over a period of time may be able to develop a church culture that encourages a direct transmission of faith from parents to their children. Many parents have expressed to me their deepest appreciation for equipping them to lead their children to Christ. As parents who led two of our children to faith in Christ, my wife and I feel that the experience is as precious as our own conversion. In addition to equipping parents in evangelistic skills, a wise pastor would want to equip his leaders who work with children and youth. Sunday school teachers, Bible study leaders, Vacation Bible School (VBS) workers, and AWANA leaders will benefit from the evangelism training as they seek to reach children for Christ.

In addition to equipping parents and children's workers, the pastor ought to lead his church to provide appropriate opportunities for children and youth to hear and embrace the good news. Some of those opportunities may include AWANA, UPWARD Sports, Children's Night, and Youth Night at evangelistic meetings. VBS has been one of the more widely used tools affording opportunities for children to hear and respond to the good news. VBS methodology has been employed effectively by many small-membership churches to reach children for Christ. As a pastor, I would typically schedule one day during VBS to speak to children about Christ in their age-appropriate settings. For those children who may be spiritually ready for a wholehearted commitment to Christ, we schedule a visit with their parents to clarify the child's spiritual readiness and provide an opportunity for parents to witness as their child makes a commitment to follow Christ as his or her Savior and Lord.

Several years ago I heard a story that motivated me to be more intentional in sharing the good news with children. D. L. Moody, an influential American evangelist, was once asked, "How many were saved tonight in that meeting?" When Moody said, two and a half, the man said, "Oh, two adults and a child?" "No," said Moody, "It was two children and an adult.

10. Fullerton, *Charles Haddon Spurgeon*, 22.

The children have their whole lives to live for Christ, while the adult has come with half of his life." Even though God values every soul regardless of the age he or she comes to faith in Christ, it is a person who comes to faith in Christ at an early age who has a potential for a lifelong kingdom service. The small church must be willing to invest time, efforts, and resources into reaching children and youth in order to reach maximum evangelistic effectiveness.

EMBRACE MASS EVANGELISM

The sixth principle for small-church evangelism embraces mass evangelism as a viable tool for reaching people with the good news. The pastor of the small church must not be afraid to use mass evangelistic events such as revival meetings. Even though the number of revival meetings in the SBC has been declining, a significant amount of churches continue to use revival meetings for evangelism and revitalization. According to one study in 1984, about 75 percent of evangelistic churches scheduled one or more revival meetings annually.[11] In another study published in 1996, slightly less than half of the evangelistic churches in the sample used local church revivals as an effective evangelistic tool.[12] According to a study conducted by the Georgia Baptist Convention in 2001, 58 percent of the churches in the state conducted a local church revival.[13] In a recent survey of top evangelistic churches in the state of Tennessee conducted by the Tennessee Baptist Mission Board, revival meeting/harvesting events were identified as being among the most often-used evangelistic events.[14] When the pastor and church leadership determine to have a mass evangelistic event such as revival meetings, several issues must be taken in consideration.[15]

When church leadership begins to sense that God is leading them to schedule a revival meeting, they need to ask what the purpose of such an event should be. Will it be primarily for evangelism or revitalization of a local congregation? The purpose will dictate a strategy for preparation. Even though a church selects the primary purpose as evangelism, it may

11. Cathey, *A New Day in Church Revivals*, 5.

12. Rainer, *Effective Evangelistic Churches*, 32.

13. North American Mission Board, *Revival Preparation Manual*, 10

14. Tennessee Baptist Convention Mission Board, "Reaching Tour," 9.

15. For a more comprehesive discussion on revival meetings, see Johnston, *Mobilizing a Great Commission Church for Harvest*, 85–96.

experience a spiritual renewal among the membership. In turn, a church with the primary purpose as revitalization may reach people for Christ along the way. A clear purpose will enable church leadership to be more proactive in matching the purpose with a strategy for preparation and resources.

Once the primary purpose is established, the church leadership should prayerfully select a revival team. I have to confess that for the first ten years as a pastor, I invited my pastor friends to preach revival meetings. However, I came to a conclusion that if I really believed that an evangelist was God's gift to the church, I should be willing to use vocational evangelists. The Conference of Southern Baptist Evangelists is a group of full-time evangelists who serve as an excellent resource for selecting leaders to preach and lead music in revival meetings. Many churches have benefited greatly from the giftedness of vocational evangelists. The meetings were blessed with people coming to Christ, and believers renewed in their faith.

Another consideration in relation to the revival teams should be clarity about finances. It has been my practice as a pastor to initiate the conversation about finances with an evangelist. Typically, we would budget the money for expenses (travel, food, lodging, and incidentals) and use a love offering to provide honorarium for the revival team. If you choose this method, make sure the love offering will be given to the team in its entirety. Some churches would budget an entire amount for expenses and honorariums. Regardless of the approach, the church leadership and the revival team must be clear about finances at the onset of the process. If the church decides to use the love offering method to reimburse the revival team, the pastor needs to plan a thoughtful and prayerful love offering. For full-time evangelists, this money is how God provides for their families. In addition, church leaders should be gracious hosts to the revival team. Church members observe how pastors and staff treat the revival team and in many instances that is how church members learn how to treat their leaders!

After the church leadership establishes the purpose and secures a spiritually gifted revival team, they are ready to develop a strategy for preparation. Many state conventions publish manuals on revival preparation. The church must begin preparations three to six months in advance. Church leadership should share enthusiastically with the church council, deacons, teachers, and other key leaders about the upcoming revival. The more church members are involved in preparation of the revival meeting, the more they will be willing to attend and invite their friends to come. Revival manuals provide concrete ways of how to involve church membership in preparation and participation in revival meetings. Attempts should be made to involve as many church members as possible in various tasks associated with revival preparation and the revival meeting itself.

One critical aspect of revival preparation is publicity. The most effective form of publicity is personal invitation. A business card with information about the event may be printed and distributed to church members to use in inviting their family, friends, co-workers, and neighbors. We have found that distributing such a card one month to two months in advance created excitement, provided focus in prayer, and gave church members a tangible way to invite others. Church media such as newsletters, worship guides, and websites should provide pertinent information about the event. Publicity via Facebook, Twitter, blogs, and other viral marketing strategies by the church and church members can generate a buzz in the community and beyond about the event.

One often-neglected aspect of revival preparation is what to do with children. In one church where I served as pastor, I became concerned about an apparent lack of participation by young couples. When asked, they responded by pointing to the fact that the church did not have anything for children during the revival week. From that day forward, in addition to the typical childcare, we provided a specialized program for children during revival services. When young couples knew that their children were taken care of spiritually, they were more inclined to participate and invite their lost friends and family members to attend.

In preparation for revival meetings, post-event follow-up should not be overlooked. Training on post-event follow-up may be incorporated into the training for commitment counselors. As commitment counselors are taught how to lead people to Christ, how to provide assurance of salvation, and explore issues of church membership, an emphasis can placed on taking accurate records of those making spiritual commitments. As soon as the revival meeting concludes, names of those who made spiritual commitments can be distributed among deacons and/or Bible Study group members for further follow-up. In the churches where I have served as pastor, we continued to baptize people who were identified as potential prospects during the event months after the conclusion of the revival meetings.

The most significant aspect of revival meetings must be prayer. A genuine revival can be brought only by God. Only God can save individuals through the Holy Spirit. As the church leadership and membership engages in prayer, they acknowledge their dependence on God. From establishing the primary purpose of the revival meeting to seeking right individuals for the revival team, from publicity to personal evangelism, from taking care of spiritual needs of children to post-event follow-up, the church leadership and membership must prioritize prayer. Church leaders should set aside personal time to pray for genuine revival in their church as well as provide opportunities for church members to pray for God's movement in their church. Among various avenues for engaging membership in prayer for revival, some churches employ cottage prayer meetings in the home of church members, while other churches open up their prayer rooms for continual prayer for revival, and some others assemble prayer chains for the purpose of praying for revival.

Although some have pronounced local church revival meetings dead, they are very much alive in many churches. It is my conviction that the effectiveness of revival meetings will depend on the stewardship of that methodology by the local church. The more churches are willing to prepare, the more they place themselves in the position before God to reach people for Christ. As a pastor of a small church and a professor at a major evangelical seminary, I can't tell the small church that they must have a revival meeting! The church must seek God's will and leadership in the matter. My point is the small church should not be afraid to employ mass evangelistic events when appropriate! The aforementioned matters such as establishment of the purpose, spiritually gifted team, publicity, adequate preparation, post-event follow-up, and priority of prayer must be addressed with other mass evangelistic events including Wild Game Suppers, Power Team Ministries, Community Widows' Banquets, etc.

Another opportunity for mass evangelism occurs every Sunday morning during a worship service. By issuing a public invitation, the preacher gives an opportunity for people in the audience to respond to the good news. It is beyond the scope of this chapter to analyze different views in relation to the public invitation,[16] but my personal conviction is that a biblical message demands a call for action. Vines and Shaddix listed and discussed the following models in calling for a response to the message: verbal appeal, physical relocation, post-meeting ministry, written record, physical gesture, and a multiple approach.[17] Not every message that the pastor preaches will be evangelistic, but every message should include an evangelistic appeal. Some messages that the Holy Spirit empowers the preacher to prepare may

---

16. For further discussion on the subject, see Alan Streett, *The Effective Invitation*.

17. Vines and Shaddix, *Power in the Pulpit*, 214–15.

dictate an appeal slanted more toward discipleship, but other messages may have more of an evangelistic orientation. When the preacher depends on the Holy Spirit in preparation as well as delivery, the Holy Spirit assists the preacher in selection of an appeal in the public invitation.

INTENTIONAL CHURCH STRATEGY FOR EVANGELISM

The seventh principle for evangelism in the small church consists of an intentional church strategy for evangelism. Many churches have fifty-two disconnected Sundays during the year. They go from Sunday to Sunday without any intentionality or continuity in evangelism. To reverse the trend, the pastor will need to look beyond one event, activity, or one service in his church for evangelistic harvest resulting in an intentional, informed, and spiritual evangelistic strategy.

The pastor should be familiar with demographic trends in the community as well as spiritual patterns of his church in order to craft an informed strategy. Several elements should be considered in an evangelistic strategy. The first element is "plowing" (Jer 4:3). Just as in agriculture where fields must be prepared for sowing, the church field must be prepared spiritually. Prayer, pursuing holiness, dependence on the Holy Spirit, and practice of spiritual disciplines place the pastor and the church in a position where the Holy Spirit is free to move. The second element is "sowing" (Ps 126:5–6; Luke 8:4–15). When the pastor and church members share the good news with their community, they are sowing the seeds of the gospel. The third element is "watering" (1 Cor 3:5–8). Once the field has been plowed and the seeds have been planted, watering and caring for the field must take place. As the pastor and the church members develop relationships with the lost and demonstrate in practical ways Christ's love for the community, cultivation of the church field takes place. "Harvesting" is the next element of an effective evangelistic strategy (John 4:34–38). The church leadership needs to think of ways during the church year that provide opportunities for the unchurched to respond to the good news. The fifth element is "multiplication" (Matt 13:1–23). When people respond to the good news and become followers of Christ, the church should provide immediate and long-term follow-up for new believers.

In bringing the elements of the strategy together, a six-to-twelve-month evangelistic calendar may be helpful. I fully recognize the impossibility of scheduling actions that rely on the Holy Spirit on the calendar;

however, many spiritual activities and events may be planned. The pastor may look at sermons to preach on the biblical mandate for evangelism as the Holy Spirit leads and place them on calendar. When the pastor schedules time to pray for the lost and for personal evangelism, intentionality and accountability for evangelism are cultivated in his own life. In the area of reaching children and youth, seasonal events such as VBS and UPWARD Sports, as well as regular ministries such as Sunday school and AWANA, will need to be added to the evangelistic calendar. Mass evangelistic events with preparation and post-event follow-up activities should be placed on the calendar.

Before and during the process of strategy and calendar planning, the pastor should be praying and depending on the Holy Spirit for insights. In addition, he should ensure that the strategy is balanced by taking into account plowing, sowing, watering, harvesting, and multiplication. Granted, the pastor will not be able to address every eventuality and complexity associated with the small church, but a workable evangelistic strategy will provide an evangelistic blueprint for his personal life and the church.

In this chapter, I have attempted to share proven principles for effective evangelism stemming from my pastoral experience in the small church. My prayer as you put these principles to work in your church is that God will create an evangelistic climate where many people become devoted followers of Jesus Christ. Perhaps one of the most important lessons I have learned from leading churches in evangelism is God blesses faithfulness and perseverance. May God help us to stay faithful and persevere in sharing the good news with the world!

BIBLIOGRAPHY

Cathey, Bill. *A New Day in Church Revivals.* Nashville: Broadman, 1984.

Fish, Roy. *Every Member Evangelism for Today.* New York: Harper and Row, 1976.

Ford, Leighton. *The Christian Persuader.* Philadelphia: Westminster, 1966.

Fullerton, W.Y. *Charles Haddon Spurgeon: A Bibliography.* Self-published, CreateSpace, 2014.

Johnston, Thomas. ed. *Mobilizing a Great Commission Church for Harvest.* Eugene, OR: Wipf & Stock, 2011.

Louisiana Baptist Convention. *One on One: Evangelism Made Simple.* Alexandria, LA: Louisiana Baptist Convention, 2017.

North American Mission Board. *Revival Preparation Manual.* Atlanta: North American Mission Board, 2009.

———. 3 *Circles Evangelism Kit.* Atlanta: North American Mission Board, 2012

Rainer, Thom. *The Bridger Generation.* Nashville: Broadman and Holman, 1997.

————. *Effective Evangelistic Churches*. Nashville: Broadman and Holman, 1996.

Reid, Alvin. *Evangelism Handbook*. Nashville: B&H Academic, 2009.

Roudkovski, Jake. "An Investigation into a Relationship between Pastoral Personal Evangelism and Baptisms in Selected Southern Baptist Churches." PhD diss., New Orleans Baptist Theological Seminary, 2004.

Spurgeon, Charles H. *Spurgeon at His Best*. Compiled by Tom Carter. Grand Rapids: Baker, 1988.

Streett, Alan. *The Effective Invitation*. Grand Rapids: Kregel, 1995.

Tennessee Baptist Convention Mission Board. "Reaching Tour: What's Working in Evangelism Today?" Forthcoming.

Vines, Jerry, and Jim Shaddix. *Power in the Pulpit: How to Prepare and Deliver Expository Sermons*. Chicago: Moody, 1997.

4

Sermon Preparation
in the Small Church

BO RICE

I t is a great privilege to pastor the local church. I've had this privilege
twice in my ministry. It is a joy to live life with a local body of Christ and
see how God does an incredible work in his people. I am convinced that
the greatest calling and joy one receives as a pastor is to preach the word
of God—to deliver the word from the Lord to his people, and see how it
has the power to change lives for the glory of God. In order to do this effectively, the preacher must be prepared. It is at this point we must realize
the work of preparing and delivering sermons is spiritual warfare. There is
a battle being waged for the preacher's mind and attention. Satan and his
legions are fighting to distract the preacher from spending time in God's
word and preparing the message that God wants his people to hear. On top
of the spiritual warfare, there are many other issues and responsibilities that
work against the preacher's time to study and prepare. While pastoring, I
learned quickly that life and ministry happen. Leading staff meetings, going on hospital visits, conducting counseling sessions are all important, but
so is preaching the word of God. It is paramount that the pastor schedule
his study time just like every other meeting he has throughout the week.

Having a good skill set in homiletics is vital to effective sermon preparation. We must learn the rules of homiletics. After learning the basic rules,
it is important we continue to practice them on a weekly basis. I encourage

you to think about your own preaching preparation. Write down what has helped you in the past. Develop your own preparation guides and outlines to follow each week. Take time to review your methods of preparation and learn from what others practice in their preparation. Understand there is no one method that is the "must do" of sermon preparation, even if it's your own way. I encourage every pastor to read as many books on preaching and preparation as you can find. I certainly do not believe I can offer much new advice to the field; however, I can share with you some of the gleanings from my own journey in sermon preparation and preaching. Below, I put forth some of the simple yet important rules of sermon preparation. I also provide some practical resources that can be used in the process.

PRAYER

The place to begin every time you prepare to preach is on your knees. Spend time praying to God to help prepare your mind. Ask him to illuminate your mind to the truths found in his word. Ask the Holy Spirit to guide you to the truth. Through prayer, repent of your sins as the text confronts the apparent and hidden sins in your life. Never cease praying as you work on the sermon, from beginning to end. And when you stand to preach, pray again. Alistair Begg said he approaches his sermon preparation by thinking himself empty, reading himself full, writing himself clear, and praying himself hot. Oh that we might have more preachers who are concerned with praying themselves hot![1]

SYSTEMATIC EXPOSITION

When it comes to weekly preparation, some of the wisest counsel I received early in my ministry was to preach through books of the Bible. As Jerry Vines and Jim Shaddix stated, "Numerous benefits surface when the truth of God's Word is exposed, especially through the systematic preaching of a Bible book."[2] Biblical literacy continues to wane in the United States. This decrease in biblical literacy has caused the task of making disciples more difficult in the local church. Pastors are faced with preaching to congregations who are less likely to have any understanding of some of the most

1. Begg et al., "Sermon Prep 101," n.p.
2. Vines and Shaddix, *Power in the Pulpit*, 32.

basic biblical stories and concepts. Vines and Shaddix stated that "this scenario leaves the preacher with two options: either resign to the generation by minimizing the role of the Bible in his preaching or determine to change the generation by systematically teaching the Scriptures. Systematic exposition, especially, enhances knowledge of the Bible."[3] A thorough exegetical study and preaching through books of the Bible help preachers to become better communicators of biblical truth and the congregation to become more knowledgeable students of the word.

A second benefit to preaching through books of the Bible is it holds the preacher accountable. The preacher is held accountable for preaching what the Bible says and not what he wants to say. Preachers who approach the sermon with serious study know that they speak from the authority of the Scripture. Staying true to expositional delivery ensures that the preacher is conveying the intended truth of every text and not from the preacher's views or opinions. Also, biblical exposition holds the preacher accountable to work diligently. It is laborious work to prepare sermons each week that hold true to the intended meaning of each text in succession. Finally, the pastor is held accountable through expositional preaching by dealing with texts that would be easy to skip over. Systematic exposition forces the pastor to faithfully deal with the full counsel of God's word.

A third benefit is relieving the pastor from worrying about what to preach. Many pastors who do not preach through books of the Bible report feelings of anxiety in finding the perfect text each week. These pastors often take the barber shop approach to preaching—listening to the latest talk, concerns, and often gossip in the community, and then finding a text that may or may not address the situation. If the preacher will commit to faithful, systematic exposition, then he knows exactly what text he will be preaching every Monday as he begins his study and preparation.

A fourth benefit to systematic exposition is appetite development in the congregation. Vines and Shaddix stated, "Systematic exposition gives people an appetite for the Word that prompts them to go home and search the Scriptures for themselves."[4] Systematic exposition encourages the congregation to become better students and even teachers of the word. This, in turn, leads to further spiritual maturity for the pastor and the congregation.

Finally, there are practical benefits to systematic exposition. This type of preaching helps the pastor plan his preaching schedule for greater

3. Ibid., 33.
4. Ibid., 36.

periods of time. Also, understanding the background to each text is much easier when you are systematically preaching through the same book each week. There is very little need to do much background study each week when you already put that time in at the beginning of your study of a particular book. This approach will save you a great deal of time as you prepare week after week.

Once you have prayerfully planned your preaching, it is time to start the weekly routine. The place to begin is reading the text over and over again. In my first preaching class in seminary, I remember my professor stressing the importance of diligently reading the text. We spent the better part of an entire class period discussing the main point of the lecture, which was to "Read! Read! Read!" As my professor stressed that day, this is not the time to pick up your commentary or sermon notes from another preacher. This is the time for you to listen to what the text says. Read the text prayerfully, asking the Holy Spirit to illuminate your mind. Read the text aloud as you walk around in your office. Read the text repeatedly as if you were attempting to memorize it (maybe you will). Allow the word of God to speak to your soul and saturate your mind.

This is a good place to begin the investigation of the text as well. As you read repeatedly from your preferred translation, begin to read other versions. This will ensure you are reading the text repeatedly with a desire to discover something new. Read through literal translations and paraphrases. Finding a good parallel Bible that has translations side by side can make this a simple task. Reading the text from many translations will often reveal words and phrases that will need to be studied further at a later point.

The next step in sermon preparation is to begin asking a couple of simple questions. The inductive study method asks four questions that will often spark the investigation of a given text. H.B. Charles Jr. comments, "The inductive Bible study method asks four big questions of the text: (1) Observation asks, What does it say? (2) Interpretation asks, What does it mean? (3) Application asks, How does it apply? And (4) Correlation asks, How does it relate to the rest of Scripture?"[5] Observation of the text is simply making notes on what you see in the text, taking note of important, repeated, or difficult words. Also, it includes asking journalistic questions like who, what, when, where, and why.

---

5. Charles Jr., *On Preaching*, 37. Charles recommends *Living by the Book: The Art and Science of Reading the Bible* by Howard and William Hendricks for a comprehensive introduction to the inductive Bible study method.

This is the time to start diagramming the text as well. Diagramming helps to understand the flow of the text. There are differing methods of diagramming. Some preachers diagram the original language; others diagram in English. Regardless of which you prefer, it is important to divide the text phrase by phrase using lines or some other method to show how the phrases connect to one another. Diagramming will help to identify the main clause and then how all corresponding clauses relate to the main. This helps to reveal the intended flow from one idea to another. Also, this will help when the time comes for developing the sermon outline.

Once you have a good idea of a text's structure, give attention to specific words and how those words relate to each other. Vines and Shaddix state, "Word studies can help the expositor determine the literal meaning of the text by revealing the simple, plain, obvious, and literal sense of the words, phrases, clauses, and sentences of the passage. Never minimize the use of a particular word."[6] Again, it is good to read through the original language as best you can. The original languages are filled with incredible word pictures. Look at every word in a particular text if possible. If the text is lengthy, focus on the main words. Take time to look up the meaning of words in the original languages by using lexical aids, theological dictionaries, and other resources like computer software. Logos is Bible software I use that provides word studies with just a few clicks. Vines and Shaddix state, "Sometimes the original meaning of a word is absolutely essential to the interpretation of the passage."[7] I would contend that it is always essential to the interpretation of the passage if the goal is faithful, text-driven preaching.

When considering particular words, it's important to determine how the word was used by the person who wrote it. Background studies often reveal particular cultural terms and idioms that are used throughout the book you are studying.

The next step in sermon preparation is to allow Scripture to interpret itself. Checking cross-references is a great way to accomplish this task. This will help you discover what other passages of Scripture say about the particular subjects that are discussed in the passage you are studying. Take time to look up word topics in an exhaustive concordance, topical Bible, or other tool such as computer software. Often, this helps to reveal truth on particular subjects in Scripture.

6. Vines and Shaddix, *Power in the Pulpit*, 112.

7. Ibid., 113.

Commentaries are a valuable resource when it comes to sermon preparation. However, it is advisable to review them later in the preparation process. Why? Vines and Shaddix state:

> The use of commentaries is mentioned last because such sources must not be allowed to sway you unduly. Our goal is to reduce subjectivity in the exegetical process as much as possible. Because commentaries are written by other human beings, they bring a high degree of subjectivity to the table.[8]

It is important to remember commentaries are not divinely inspired. Yet, it is good to learn from the wisdom of others. Make sure to get a large selection of commentaries. There should be balance in commentaries that are exegetical/critical, homiletical, and devotional. Charles Jr. says, "Read exegetical commentaries for insights into the text. Read homiletical commentaries with a view toward shaping the text for the pulpit. Read devotional commentaries to get at the heart of the text for application."[9] David Allen provides a great resource I encourage every preacher to consider when searching for different commentaries.[10]

The next step is to develop the outline of the sermon. Mark Dever and Greg Gilbert discuss the importance of developing an exegetical and preaching outline in *Preach: Theology Meets Practice*:

> The outline is a hugely important part of the sermon. It's what gives your congregation "handles" to grasp as you're preaching, and it helps them track along with you as you speak. Without a solid, clear outline, a sermon can easily become just a smooth, undifferentiated mass of words; and your listeners, not having any handles to hold to, will tune out until you're done. Not only that, but a good outline can serve to focus a sermon like a laser. Every point builds on and reinforces the last, until the whole sermon comes together powerfully to drive home one or two simple points. If you've done your outline well, your congregation should

---

8. Ibid., 118.

9. Charles Jr., *On Preaching*, 38.

10. David Allen, *Preaching Tools: An Annotated Survey of Commentaries and Preaching Resources for Every Book of the Bible*. Southwestern Seminary recently launched a new website (www.preachingsource.com), which offers many valuable resources as well. Also, New Orleans Baptist Theological Seminary plans to launch the Adrian Rogers Center for Expository Preaching where resources will be available.

be able to write down only your main points and come away with
a really good idea of what your sermon was about.[11]

Dever and Gilbert both stress the importance of working toward a
preaching outline through an exegetical outline. They argue the first step
of outlining the text is "to put down on paper, in the plainest possible language, the main ideas of our text in the order they appear. That doesn't have
to be complicated. Sometimes it's just a few sentences that give a snapshot
of what's going on in the text."[12] The exegetical outline does not need to be
lengthy. It simply needs to capture the shape and main point(s) of the text
you are about to preach.

The purpose of the exegetical outline is to lead you to a preaching
outline. The preaching outline contains the actual points you will articulate
to your congregation when you preach the sermon. The preaching outline
is moving from the exegetical outline of "a bare statement of what the text
says and means to a more pointed 'firing' of that text to the hearts and
minds of your congregation."[13] The preaching outline should begin with
a single sentence or two of the main idea of the sermon. Obviously, this
should come from the main idea of the text. Haddon Robinson calls this
the Exegetical Idea, Vines and Shaddix call this the Central Idea of the Text,
and Harold Bryson labeled it the Essence of a Text in a Sentence.[14] Vines
and Shaddix state, "To do the necessary word study, to gather the needed
background data, and to study the contextual considerations is not difficult.
But to pull together in one succinct statement the essence of a paragraph of
Scripture can be a most rigorous assignment."[15] Yet, this is a necessary step
in preparing to preach. The entire sermon should be an extension of the
main or central idea.

Once you have discovered the main idea of the text and settled on the
main idea of the sermon, it is important to begin working through the ob-
jectives of the sermon (what you want the congregation to think, feel, do).
This will help as you continue to develop your outline. As Charles Jr. states,
"Put the structure together before you try to put meat on the bones."[16]

11. Dever and Gilbert, *Preach*, 86.

12. Ibid., 86.

13. Ibid., 88.

14. Robinson, *Biblical Preaching*, 31-70; Vines and Shaddix, *Power in the Pulpit*, 128-
33; Bryson, *Expository Preaching*, 316.

15. Vines and Shaddix, *Power in the Pulpit*, 129.

16. Charles Jr., *On Preaching*, 39

Now comes the point where many busy pastors think they are ready to preach. However, I have always found value in taking my sermon preparation to the next level by writing a complete sermon manuscript. There are many who argue against the use of a manuscript during the preaching event. I certainly would agree that a preacher should not read his manuscript from the pulpit. At the same time, writing a manuscript has always helped me feel more prepared to accurately and adequately handle the word of God. Charles Jr. says,

> If you develop your sermon skeleton (outline) carefully, you may be tempted to slap an introduction and conclusion on it and declare yourself ready to preach. Resist that temptation. Take the time to write out a complete, word-for-word manuscript. This will help you think through and fully develop your ideas, and allow you to absorb the sermon into your memory. You may not take the manuscript to the pulpit. In fact, I recommend you don't. You should prepare a brief set of notes for preaching. But these pulpit notes should be pared down from a complete sermon manuscript.[17]

This is wise advice for the busy pastor. There is great value in thinking through the entirety of your sermon and writing a manuscript helps with this process.

As you write the manuscript, be sure to write with your listeners in mind. Imagine yourself speaking the words to your intended audience as you write them. Be sure to write in plain terms. Remember that your audience often will not have the same background and study time of the text like you. Be sure to follow the sermon outline you developed to stay focused on the intended truth while figuring out the best way to convey the message.

The beginning and ending of a sermon are two of the most critical points in the delivery. The introduction should grab the audience's attention while building interest in the central idea. While writing the manuscript, you should clearly state the point of the message in the introduction. Also, keep it brief. Charles Jr. states:

> You want to spend the bulk of your time explaining and applying the text. So get to the point quickly. Don't ramble. Don't waste words. Don't loiter on the front porch. You can undermine yourself by taking too much time to tell a story, build suspense, or make an application, leaving limited time to deal with the text.[18]

17. Ibid., 39.
18. Ibid., 82.

The beginning and end are important, but how you say what's in the middle is as well. Give special attention to transitional statements. Your transitions should be smooth while helping your audience follow your train of thought. When you come to the conclusion, be sure to end with purpose. Too often, preachers come to the end with little time left and even less thought as to what to say. End by summarizing the main point and calling the people to action. Robinson recognizes there are many ways to end the sermon with purpose. He encourages the use of a summary, illustration, quotation, question, prayer, or giving specific directions to the audience. Regardless of the form, Robinson believes "these final moments should drive home what has been said, and they must not take the audience off into new avenues of thought. The sermon itself moves the gun into position; now is the time to fire the shot at the listener's mind and emotions."[19]

As you work on your manuscript, this is where you begin to develop application and illustration. John Broadus stated, "Application, in the strict sense, is that part, or those parts, of the discourse in which it is shown how the subject applies to the persons addressed, what practical instructions it offers them, what practical demands it makes upon them."[20] The preacher has the tremendous responsibility of helping link the truth of the text with the hearers' need. Greg Gilbert uses an "Application Grid" to help him think through the application of a text. The grid contains questions that can help with application:

- How does the teaching in this point fit into the salvation-historical progression of the biblical story line?
- What does this text say to the non-Christian?
- What does it say to the larger society and to policy-makers?
- What does it say about Jesus?
- How does it apply to the individual Christian?
- Does it say anything in particular about issues of work or family?
- What does it say to my own local church?[21]

---

19. Robinson, *Biblical Preaching*, 171.

20. Broadus, *On the Preparation and Delivery of Sermons,* 167 (page citation is to the revised edition).

21. Dever and Gilbert, *Preach*, 93.

As I have considered application throughout the years, I always ask, "What does this text say to my people? What does it say to those who are listening today? And what are they to do with this truth now?"

Illustrations are a valuable resource in making clear the intended meaning of a text. The word "illustrate" comes from the Latin *illustrare*, which means "to cast light upon." In this regard, illustrations serve as windows in a house. Charles Spurgeon said "illustrations are like windows because they brighten the sermon with light just like the window does for the home."[22] It is essential at this point in preparation that the preacher thinks of ways to enhance his message with additional light. Vines and Shaddix contend that good illustrations can mean the difference between an average sermon and an outstanding sermon. They state that illustrations serve five primary purposes: illustrations clarify, intensify, apply, attract, and argue the intended truth.[23] A great concern of using illustrations is how to do so effectively. Danny Aiken, Bill Curtis, and Stephen Rummage offer a simple, yet extensive list for using illustrations in the sermon:

1. *Avoid using too many illustrations.* Your primary task is to expound the Scriptures, not to tell stories.

2. *Use, but do not abuse, personal illustrations.* Your sermon is about Jesus, not about you.

3. *Seek variety.* Routines can create ruts. Avoid getting into one.

4. *Represent the truth.* Be honest, tell the truth, and make it credible. Avoid misrepresenting the truth.

5. *Avoid using illustrations in bad taste.* Always follow the rule of speaking with modesty and decency.

6. *Never use counseling situations without prior permission.* It violates confidences and can slap you with a lawsuit.

7. *Master the art of using illustrations.* Learn to do it well.

8. *Avoid announcing the illustration.* If you have to announce it, you probably have a poor illustration.

9. *Make sure it has life!* Visualize the story in your mind. Get into it and tell it from the inside out.

10. *Avoid overusing a particular illustration (especially in the same church).*

22. Spurgeon, *Lectures to My Students*, 349.
23. Vines and Shaddix, *Power in the Pulpit*, 191.

11. *Avoid using illustrations as mere decorations or fillers to take up time.* You should be better prepared and more serious about your assignment.

12. *Be sure the illustration works well!* If it does not, then do not use it.

13. *Be vivid.* Learn how to tell a story well. Some are gifted at telling stories; others have to work at it.

14. *Develop a sense of humor that is natural to you.*

15. *Practice the dramatic.* It is no sin to study from and learn from actors who excel at this art.

16. *Avoid using canned, trite, commonplace, and overused illustrations.* Throw away those illustration books you bought. You do not need them.

17. *Avoid using an illustration simply to play on people's emotions.* Pull on but do not trample on their feelings. Playing on people's emotions is another component of ministerial malpractice.

18. *Keep the occasion and congregation in mind.* What works in one place may not fit in another (especially in a different country or culture).

19. *Avoid making fun of anyone other than yourself.* Ridiculing others is homiletical suicide and will destroy credibility with your audience.

20. *Always give credit for borrowed illustrations.* It is a shame we even need to make this point.[24]

It is important to give illustrations this special attention. Spurgeon taught his students that "it is a great pity when illustrations are so confused as both to darken the sense and create diversion. Muddled metaphors are muddles indeed; let us give the people good illustrations or none at all."[25] Practice the tips listed above while using illustrations and see how truth is illumined in the minds of your people.

Once all the sermon preparation is complete and notes from your manuscript are in hand, your work is still not done. We must end where we began: on our knees. Dear pastor, I implore you to pray before, while, and after you prepare. Pray before you stand to preach. Pray as soon as you are done preaching. Bathe yourself, your preparation, and your preaching in prayer! Then trust the Lord to use his word in and through you.

24. Akin, Curtis, and Rummage, *Engaging Exposition*, 168–69.
25. Spurgeon, *Lectures to My Students*, 361.

In the appendices, you will find several practical resources to use during your sermon preparation. The "Diagram of the Text" and "Observations of the Text" pages are adapted from Wayne McDill's 12 *Essential Skills for Great Preaching*.[26] I offer the variation to show the resources I have used throughout the years to develop sermons. The "Sermon Outline" is the same as the one used in the Preaching Practicum course at New Orleans Baptist Theological Seminary. There are many other examples that can be found with a simple search of the internet and other preaching resources. However, these are the ones I have used regularly.

Again, I encourage you to gather as many sources on preaching and preparation as you can find. Understand that your call to preach is a call to prepare. That call to prepare never grows old; neither should your learning. You will also find a selected bibliography in the appendices that offers many great resources on sermon preparation. This list is extensive, yet not exhaustive.

BIBLIOGRAPHY

Akin, Daniel L., et al. *Engaging Exposition*. Nashville: B & H Academic, 2011.

Allen, David. *Preaching Tools: An Annotated Survey of Commentaries and Preaching Resources for Every Book of the Bible*. Fort Worth, TX: Seminary Hill, 2016.

Begg, Alistair, et al. "Sermon Prep 101 with Alistair Begg, Bryan Chapell, and Mike Bullmore." https://www.truthforlife.org/blog/sermon-prep-101-alistair-begg-and-bryan-chapel/.

Broadus, John A. *On the Preparation and Delivery of Sermons*. 4th ed. Revised by Vernon L. Stanfield. New York: Harper & Row, 1979.

Bryson, Harold. *Expository Preaching: The Art of Preaching Through a Book of the Bible*. Nashville: B & H, 1995.

Charles Jr., H.B. *On Preaching: Personal & Pastoral Insights for the Preparation & Practice of Preaching*. Chicago: Moody, 2014.

Dever, Mark, and Greg Gilbert. *Preach: Theology Meets Practice*. Nashville: B & H Academic, 2012.

Robinson, Haddon. *Biblical Preaching: The Development and Delivery of Expository Messages*. Grand Rapids: Baker, 1980.

Spurgeon, Charles. *Lectures to My Students*. Grand Rapids: Zondervan, 1954.

McDill, Wayne. *12 Essential Skills for Great Preaching*, 2nd ed. Revised and expanded. Nashville: B & H Academic, 2006.

Vines, Jerry, and Jim Shaddix. *Power in the Pulpit*. Chicago: Moody, 1997.

26. McDill, 12 *Essential Skills for Great Preaching*, p. 35 for his structural diagram table and p.49 for his immediate observations table.

5

Worship Leadership within the Small Church

Ed Steele

INTRODUCTION

At the seminary, I am constantly in contact with pastors or committee chairs looking for a worship leader and have heard a grocery list of requests, some complaints, and a host of urgent pleas. Just this week I was having lunch with one of our young men who is planting a multiethnic congregation and listening to the stories of his struggles as they are three months into their launching and already have over thirty people who are active. "We don't have anyone who can play the guitar or keyboard, we just sing with videos when we meet together." He went on to share the negative and positive responses he had received about some of the songs which had been used in their worship services. Frustration. Struggle. "What can we do?" he asked, sincerely looking for help. Granted, his might be an exception, but one of the common issues the leadership of smaller congregations has to face is the lack of trained leaders in the area of music and worship. While there is no one answer to this issue since all churches are different, I do believe there is help available and some principles that can inform us as we deal with the many challenges of worship leadership.

FOUNDATIONS

I live in south Louisiana, literally in and around the land that years ago was a swamp. Every building here must have support columns under its foundation, which is common. What is not common is these columns never are driven down to the bedrock, because the bedrock is hundreds of feet below the surface. In addition, the ground is constantly settling so that every few years I have to add soil to the lawn and surrounding area around the foundation of the house to avoid exposure. Can you imagine how long a building would stand if it didn't have those columns under the foundations?

Before we launch into the subject of worship leadership we need to lay down some strong columns upon which to place the foundations for what needs to be presented. We base our decisions on one or more of the following columns: God's word, history and tradition, human intellect, and personal experience.[1] Scripture is our ultimate and final source of authority. Regardless of what we might think, or how we might have done things in the past, or even logically believe, we can never bypass the teachings of God's word. History and tradition inform our worldview and help us avoid having to reinvent the wheel every time we do something, but it is possible that over time the original reason for which we did something no longer exists and has lost its meaning. For example, in rural areas farmers had to milk cows and other chores daily, so when Sunday came around they had to complete their work before they could go to church. By the time they could get there it was around 11:00 a.m., however nowhere in Scripture does it say we need to start worship at 11:00.

The ability to deduce and make logical deductions is a gift from God, but we must remember we are of Adam's race and have "clay feet" that is, we have the ability to come to the wrong conclusions. I am reminded of an incident in which engineers lost a $125-million-dollar Mars orbiter because they had used English units of measurement, rather than the standard metric system. In the case of a conflict of our logical conclusions and the word of God, Scripture always must take precedence. Personal experience is an important teacher, as anyone who has picked up a hot frying pan without a pot holder will testify. However, using personal experience that is not consistent with the teachings of God's word can lead to disastrous results.

---

1. Known also as the *Wesleyan Quadrilateral*, a fuller discussion of these is found in their relationship to worship in Steele, *Worship HeartCries*, 1-6.

So what? What difference does this make related to leadership and worship? I'm glad you asked. When trouble, conflict, or questions arise we need to ask ourselves, "From which of the four is this based?" When someone says to me, "We've always done it that way!" more than likely they are basing their decision on history and tradition. While not necessarily wrong, then change would not be in violation unless their current method is taught in Scripture. Personal opinion and past experience can be helpful, but should never be in violation of what is taught in God's word.

The reason we have invested this much time so far with this issue is many of those in our congregations are unclear as to what the Bible teaches about worship. They know what they have done in the past, they know what they like from personal experience, but have never immersed themselves in the study and application of the biblical teachings about worship. Since there are many good sources in this area, I will only give a basic biblical definition of worship. Worship is our obedient response to the revealed nature and character of God. Worship is not dependent on how we might feel but on our obedient response. Worship is not dependent on our likes and dislikes, for the goal of worship is not to please me, but to please God. Worship is not for our entertainment, but for our transformation. Once we can settle what worship is and begin to live in that reality, then many of these other issues will fall by the wayside.

One model of worship is worth mentioning here; it is not the only one, but will be helpful to us here and for the next section as we look at planning. The prophet Isaiah's vision in chapter 6 is well known and does describe how God calls him into the prophetic ministry he would have for the rest of his life. Since entire books are written on this one chapter, I will only give a few summary statements that relate to its application to worship.

Implicit is the fact that God initiates worship: he was there giving the vision, for we do not ask God to come to meet with us, he is calling us to meet with him. God is the initiator. The bush was burning before Moses saw it; he did not invoke God's presence and neither do we. We do not plead and beg for the Spirit of God to come among us; he already lives within the lives of those who know Christ as Savior and Lord. God is already present waiting on us.

Isaiah mentions that he "saw the Lord, high and lifted up," that he was holy, holy, holy, or in the language of the Old Testament, three times holy—the holiest possible. God revealed his nature and character. It must have been a breathtaking moment for the prophet. Isaiah did not invoke the presence of God; God simply revealed himself. Immediately after this revelation of God's character, the prophet saw himself as God did—a sinner, unclean, living among an unclean people. From this revelation of his own nature, Isaiah confesses his sin and that of his people and is forgiven, symbolized by the touching of the live coal to the prophet's lips and at the same time placing the blazing message of God upon them. What follows is crucial if we desire to understand worship from this passage. Verse eight begins with the phrase, "*Then* I heard the voice of the Lord." Stop. Go back over that again. "*Then* I heard." The ability to hear and understand God's voice was dependent on what had happened before: God's revealing of his nature and character, Isaiah's recognition and confession of sin, and God's grace and forgiveness. Then he was able to hear God speaking. I sincerely believe one of the reasons the members of our churches do not worship is not because God is not there, but that they have never come to the point of a *then* in their lives: seeing God, seeing themselves, confessing sin, and accepting the forgiveness God is offering.

However, Isaiah's experience did not end there. The prophet responded to God's question: "Whom shall I send, and who will go for us?" The experience was not complete until the prophet responded obediently to God's voice. The measure of our worship is not the depth of our feelings in the service, but the obedient response to all God is commanding. Worship completes itself in obedient response. Now that we have laid some foundations, let's move on to see how all these things fit together.

HELP BEHIND THE DESK: PLANNING

Once we understand what worship is, we are confronted with the process of planning for that time together as a congregation seeking to practice what we believe. What are some of the questions with which we must wrestle in this process? Who is involved in planning the worship? How do we determine what we should do? What should the person[s] involved be called? Where can I get help? What should we do if we don't have anyone to lead, or play, etc.? These questions are important and must be answered, but before we attempt an answer, let me address one issue that is sometimes overlooked.

While many small congregations have a Minister of Music, Worship Leader, or Worship Pastor, the fact of the matter is the senior pastor is the primary leader of worship. The congregation notices if he is participating in the singing, giving, praying, the fellowship of the service, or using the time to go over the notes one more time. The truth is we cannot take our people where we have not been. While the primary responsibility for planning and leading the congregational worship may be left to another individual, it is of great importance that the under-shepherd of the flock set an example that corporate worship is a vital part of his life and ministry.

Who is Involved in Planning the Worship?

Ideally, the pastor gives the vision and direction for the service based on sh the passage chosen for the message.[2] Ideally, if preaching through a book or topical series, as much information as possible should be shared with the person or group that will be leading the worship service. Unfortunately, in many of our smaller churches, there isn't a leadership group to take hold of the planning, but generally one person who is doing most of the planning based on the skills he or she has and knowledge of the available resources. Many times, because the pastor is the only full-time employee of the church, long-range sermon planning is only a dream he had in Seminary, and instead he feverishly works out two to three messages every week between hospital visits, committee meetings, squabbles, not to mention the issues of his own family.

What can be done, then? In the situation mentioned above, the first thing for the pastor to do would be to stop and pray, and I don't mean that facetiously. I know you are praying about it and that it has been a concern. We know we are already doing too much, but really don't know how to stop the train. I personally have been helped by Peter Scazzero's book, *The Emotionally Healthy Leader*. Prayer helps us refocus on our priorities and helps us hear from God. Another help is to have a worship planning team that consists of two or more individuals involved in the worship ministry who are willing to work together. Other times, there is just a volunteer who is the worship leader, who should work with the pastor in the planning process.

Collecting the Tools

A worship service generally is comprised of various aspects of worship: the reading of God's word, prayers, offerings, singing and other forms of

2. McKeever, "The Pastor Is the Worship Leader," n.p.

music, Communion, etc., which have been a part of worship since the early church. Each should play an important part of our obedient response to God, and not just be considered something to be done for tradition's sake. While no specific order is given in Scripture, it does not mean that we throw organization out the window. "Unity and flow" are keys words in the worship planning process that can be of great help to those charged with that responsibility. "Unity" means that the various pieces fit together like the pieces of a puzzle to reveal a complete picture. All that is said, done, and sung is in harmony with each other and the message from God's word. "Flow" entails connected progression; that is, each song, prayer, or other part of the service links to the others without breaking the spirit of the service, climaxing toward an obedient response to the moving of God's Spirit revealed from his word. Some services lend themselves to a high-energy, upbeat beginning and gradually come together for a meditative focus on the passage to be preached. Others begin with a low-key meditative start and gradually move toward a celebration in the message.

One important word of caution: with the increasing availability of worship resources and songs from the internet, great attention must be given to the text of the songs being used for the service. While the use of hymnals may seem outdated, they did have some guarantee that the theology of the text of the songs had been reviewed by a group of theologians before publication. However, that theological filter has been removed and one must realize not all songs that are available (and even publically popular on Christian radio and other media outlets) contain solid biblical doctrine. The texts of many of these songs can (and should) be changed to correct them, otherwise we will be teaching and reinforcing wrong doctrine among believers. The measure of a song is not how popular it is on the charts, nor who has recorded it, but the veracity of the doctrine taught and its singability by the congregation.

Theme

When planning a worship service, first ask yourself, "What is the purpose of this particular service? What is the theme? Around what text are we building and utilizing the various elements of worship?" Until you have answered these questions, you are not ready to plan. Knowing the central theme of the message is crucial to good planning.

Even if the specifics of the message are not known, something as simple as knowing that the pastor is preaching through one of the gospels, like the Gospel of John, can be of enormous help to the person who is planning worship. Even though this is not a detailed outline of where the pastor will be week by week (though this may come in time), it is a good starting point and can greatly aid in the planning process. For example, if there is a small choir or praise team, it takes time to put music together that might go well with the message. So a key element of the planning process is to have a point of departure in terms of the topic.

Resources

Once the theme is known, then gather around you the planning resources you have available: Bible, hymnal (for the topical reference and biblical references in the indices), Song Select from CCLI (if a member; fee is tied to the size of the congregation), other music collections and helps like Life-WayWorship.com. Most pastors have an idea of an order of worship and the elements they wish to include, so knowing this ahead of time will save hours in the future. Changing the order, especially one that has existed for quite some time can be done, but only with thoughtful reflection and not just "change for change's sake." As the saying goes, "never pull up a fence until you know why it was put there in the first place; what it was keeping out may come back and bite you."

Putting Together the Pieces

Let's follow the idea of preaching through the Gospel of John and suppose that the first message centers on "In the beginning was the Word and the Word was with God and the Word was God . . . " The theme could go a number of directions: God's word, Christ's Incarnation, the Trinity, and so on, but we'll go with God's word. To gather some musical resources we can begin searching the LifeWayWorship.com site on "God's Word, & Bible." When I did, I came up with many more options for songs than I could possibly use in one service, so I picked a few from the past and present: "Word of God Speak," "Speak O Lord," "How Firm a Foundation," "Ancient Words," just for starters. (A thought: Don't just use the songs you already know; be willing to learn new songs or older songs that are new to you.) Most likely the congregation knows some songs you do not and you know some they do not. Experience will help learn what is known and what is not.

Let's look at some other elements: is there a video clip from GodTube. com you might use, or what about a related passage that the congregation could read together? What about a testimony of someone for whom memorizing Scripture has changed their life? What about prayers? The offering? Other musical elements from a group, etc.? Will Communion be celebrated as part of the service? Notice that announcements have not been included, since they aren't really a part of worship. Put them in a bulletin or give them before or after the service; keep the service centered on worship.

Using the order that the pastor, you, or the worship team have developed, then begin to piece together the various elements with "unity and flow." Some musical knowledge is necessary to be able to tie songs together, so don't be ashamed to seek help if you are weak in that area. Your musicians will greatly appreciate it and the music will flow from one song to another. You may want an opening section or set of songs to begin the service and another before and/or after. You may want to connect these songs with prayers, video clips, testimonies, and offerings, or other elements you and the pastor have chosen. Be sensitive to the amount of time what you have planned will take: if your service is only an hour long and what you have planned takes up forty-five minutes, then you have cut the pastor's time to preach or have forced him to go over. Work out first with the pastor how much time he needs for his sermon, then work from there. Remember you are not in competition, but working together.

What if that is not possible? What if the pastor is not able to plan that far ahead, how can those that plan worship plan for something they know nothing about? Great question. Just because the person leading worship does not have the pastor's outline, does not mean the service being planned is done without continuity. With the same prayerful leadership, the worship leader should seek to plan a service in which everything that is done connects together and is built around a theme. Better to plan a worship service ahead of time and work out the details of the theme and transitions than to try to throw something together at the last minute, expecting the musicians to play well without having time to practice and work out any problems.

Introducing a new song: So many new songs are being written that it is possible to have a service in which every song is new every week. Though that may be possible, it is not desirable. Most musicians love to learn and add as many new songs as possible, however, the average congregation cannot process that many new songs so quickly. A song must be sung several times over a period of weeks before it can really become part of a canon of songs the church members can sing from the heart. If all they hear is new songs, the congregation will never have an opportunity to internalize and memorize the song so it becomes part of their lives. When teaching a new song, it is more effective to have it sung as a solo, then repeated with the congregation. Avoid introducing more than one new song per week; in fact, one new song per week might be too much for some congregations. Introduce the song in different ways: have children or youth sing it as a musical offering during the service; most adults love to hear them sing and the first impression of the song will be positive. Play recordings of the song as pre-service music. Be creative, but keep the emphasis on worship.

What should we do if we don't have anyone to lead, or play, etc.? Lack of accompanists seems to be one of the most common issues I have come across during the last several years, and one of the most difficult to correct. Becoming skillful enough to accompany others is not something that happens overnight. Some options might be [1] check the local high school or home school group to see if there are those that can play a keyboard or guitar, [2] be willing to pay for lessons for a church member to learn, [3] sing with pre-recorded music, or [4] sing without any instruments. Make it a matter of prayer. While the decline of public school music programs has exacerbated the problem of children learning music, many churches have begun music academies where private music lessons are offered. There might be a church in the area with one of these academies in which the church could offer to sponsor a student that would be able to aid in the music part of the service.

HELP FROM BEHIND THE PULPIT: PARTICIPATION

Let me crack open the door of my office long enough so you can overhear the questions that have been raised over the years from pastors and worship leaders: "Although our small congregation makes a 'joyful noise' (and sometimes, not so joyful) how can we get them to sing? Many never even open their mouths." "We really don't have any real singers in our group, so after the time of singing, it is really difficult for the pastor to preach." "Our little praise team consists of two or three loving brothers and sisters with good intentions, but their efforts really do little to inspire worship. What can we do?"

I wish I had a magic wand and could whisk away these issues with a simple flick of the wrist, but I don't. Several issues that need to be addressed if we are to get to the root of this problem, but I will mention only four: [1] What is the role of the music leadership? [2] How can we improve the leadership we have? [3] Does our congregation (and the present leadership) understand what worship is and music's role in it? [4] What makes a song congregational?

What is the Role of the Music leadership?

A question that is implicit within that question is "What is the role of music in worship?" If we can answer that, then we will be in better shape to answer the other. Music is a tool to facilitate worship, whether by being the vehicle through which praise and adoration are shared (sung or strictly instrumental), or whether it is the means by which truth is taught through the text of the songs. The role of music leadership is the coordination and facilitation of the music used in worship and training in the development of future music leadership. A worship leader model that does not include the mentoring for future leadership is short-sighted and can become self-focused.

How can We Improve the Leadership We have?

Each leader must honestly evaluate both their knowledge of worship and skill level in leading and playing. Until a leader is willing to acknowledge what may be lacking, there will be little hope for improvement. Many schools and seminaries have certificate programs, associate and bachelor degrees that focus on both worship studies (sometimes by distance learning) and skill development. Wise is the congregation that is willing to invest in the development of its leadership by providing a scholarship for the leader. Wise is the leader who is not satisfied with just doing enough to get by, but is committed to lifelong learning and sharing what has been learned.

Does Our Congregation (and Leadership) Understand what Worship is and Music's Role in it?

Learning how to teach the congregation what worship is and isn't is an ongoing process; it is not a one-time sermon on worship or a workshop.

One of the reasons Israel fell into idol worship during the period of the Judges was the fathers failed to teach their children and the ongoing process of retelling God's workings was abandoned. Some resources for study are mentioned in the appendices and I suggest a yearly study or emphasis for the leadership as a minimum, or better yet for the entire congregation. Studies such as these can help prevent the church and leadership from falling into the "performance and entertainment" and "everything must please me" mentalities which are prevalent in some of today's churches.

What Makes a Song Congregational?[3]

Many times I have looked out over a congregation and noticed that some are not singing or drop out during parts of a song that is out of their range. Many of the contemporary songs were written by composers/singers whose range is very wide, much wider than the average person in the pew. When a worship leader uses one of these songs in the same key as the original the result can be less than what was desired. Most congregations cannot sing above a D [4th line] or Eb [4th space], but many of the songs go way beyond those norms resulting in the singers having to yell, scream, or drop out completely. A simple solution is to sing the song in a lower key. Worship leadership should practice this ahead of time to work out what can and cannot be done. Some songs really are better for a praise team to sing, rather than the congregation because of their rhythmic complexity or difficulty. Forcing a song on a congregation that it cannot sing well will only cause frustration and the intended message of the text will probably be lost in the shuffle. Leading implies someone following, so worship leadership must always be aware and sensitive to what is going on in the congregation, for if the congregation is not following, the worship team is not truly leading.

One other word about participation in worship. It would be wise to recall what was said about introducing a new song in a previous section. We do not just plan to throw together some old songs and new songs just to make everyone happy. The goal of worship is to present a sacrifice of praise that is pleasing to God, not just to satisfy personal tastes. Worship is always God-centered. At the same time, we must speak the language understood by those who are in the congregation. Sometimes a specific theme may require more new songs than older hymns, or older songs than new ones.

3. For further information see the blog article on the subject: http://www.edsteel-eworship.com/2010/03/what-makes-song-congregational.html.

The principle of "unity and flow" is crucial. Sometimes the worship leader may need to learn some new songs or some older ones to be able to lead effectively. The worship leaders should not be limited to their personal tastes nor working knowledge of songs, but must continually be willing to grow.

HELP ON THE OTHER SIDE OF THE PLUGS: TECHNOLOGY

The use of multimedia and technology is virtually assumed in worship. Whether one is talking about video projection of the text of the songs and sermon outline, Scripture readings, video clips, keyboards, midi instruments, iPads, or other tablets, their use is so common they may hardly be called innovative any longer. A large number of our students pull out their phones to follow along during the reading of Scripture, especially since they can easily change to the version that the chapel speaker is using that day. One survey revealed that one-third of churches use video clips, 92 percent indicate Facebook was the most effective social media platform, 74 percent read the Bible electronically, and 78 percent use cloud-based management.[4] What are some do's and don'ts related to using technology in worship?

Discover your needs first, then investigate the technologies necessary to meet those needs. Learning how to ask the right questions before you invest in technology can save thousands of dollars and much frustration. The most expensive system may or may not be the best for your specific situation or circumstance. Here are some basic questions to start, but please realize you will probably need to ask many more.

Projection Systems

What size room will be used? The distance from the projector to the screen or wall is crucial to the size of the projected image. There are short-throw projectors, but they do have limitations.

How many lumens [brightness]*will be needed?* If the room you are using has a lot of ambient light, a higher lumens projector will be needed. Generally, 3,500–6,000 lumens would fit a room that seats less than 300; projectors with greater than 6,000 are generally for larger areas.

---

4. Readings, "10 Church Technology Stats that will Astound You," n.p.

Where will it be mounted? Easily accessible power supply? Wireless or network operated? Easy access to replace bulb? Where can I get it serviced; locally or does it have to be shipped? I will not get into brands, as models change; the best advice is to research several and talk to others about their experience with them.

Projection Software

Included, but not listed is a desktop or laptop computer that will host the projection software. I will not take the time here, but it is imperative that before you buy the software you make sure the computer you have or are going to purchase has the memory and speed necessary to properly run the program. Many of these programs require high-end graphics cards and lots of RAM, so get that information first. The most common software programs are the following: PowerPoint, Easy Worship, and ProPresenter. There are many others, but these are probably the most common in use.

Microsoft Powerpoint: The most basic, each slide will have to be created, but most likely already available.

Easy Worship: Fairly easy to learn, comes with a database of song texts, Bibles, and backgrounds, as well as the ability to import videos, etc.

ProPresenter: Higher-end presentation software with even more features than Easy Worship.

One question that needs to be asked before the purchase is: "Who will be operating the software?" It very well may be that one of your middle school youth will end up as your video tech, so keep in mind who will be operating the system before you buy. Many of these programs have online video tutorials that are very helpful.

A word of caution for those using video clips: always preview and practice the use of live media in worship. Simply attaching a link to a YouTube video will most often be preceded by commercial ads that will certainly be out of place in worship, or worse yet, embarrassing. In addition, if the video is just a link, the side view will contain "related" and sponsored videos, most of which will have nothing in common with your theme and may in fact be of questionable nature. The best way to avoid this catastrophe is to download the video as a separate file and embed it in your presentation or open the link before the service starts, get past the advertisements and expand to full screen. You will also need to be ready to close the link immediately at the end, lest other videos or ads appear.

Sound Systems

What will be the main use? Just preaching? Praise band? While most people can make an adequate decision from informed reading and research on projectors and projection software, I would suggest you not try to purchase a sound system without professional consultation. Budget will likely be a major issue and it is too easy to spend thousands of dollars on things you don't need, but don't realize until later. A typical system will include at least the following: microphones (because a paper could be written on this topic alone, I defer to your consultant, but wireless is preferred for those who will be mobile on the platform area, and wired for those not having to move around), amplification and speakers (the size, kind, and location are best determined by a sound tech who can see your actual space), and sound board (here you have a choice between digital and analog, and your sound tech will be a vital source of help.) Remember, like in other situations, ask yourself, "Who is going to run this system?" Be sure whoever installs the system is willing to train several people. It would be advisable to record the training to use whenever you need to train others or review specific details.

Lighting

Here is another area where local technicians who can actually see the worship space are needed. Besides the houselights, spotlights, floodlights, and backlights, colors are only part of what needs to be considered and all must start with the question, "What do we need lighting for?" One observation I have read in some blogs and articles: care must be taken in how the platform and worship space is used, because the more it resembles a concert and performance stage, the more the congregation will approach it with that mentality; that is, whatever is happening on stage is there for my pleasure, not to facilitate congregational participation and worship.

Video for Podcasts and Websites

If services, sermons, etc. are to be recorded for podcasts, be sure your sound tech consultant is aware of this and can advise on this as well. Although there are many companies that offer turnkey website hosting, it is never as simple as advertised and training will certainly be needed to learn how to upload and maintain the web presence. If the church is going to have a website, it is imperative that it be maintained with current information and those that operate it must know the legal ramifications of what should and should not be posted. For example, to be able to use pictures of church members or children, permission must be obtained in writing. Wisdom must dictate what, if any, personal information is given out about staff or any other member since this might possibly be seen by anyone in the world.

Social Media

Twitter and Facebook are the most popular, but certainly not the only options; two other popular options are Snapchat and Instagram. Linkedin is more of a site for professional connections rather than social media. Before you jump in, always ask: "What do I wish to accomplish with this and is this the most effective use of the investment of time, resources, and people involved?" Social media can be an effective tool for announcements, but also an enormous time-waster if one is not careful in time management. Seek wise help in setting up a site for the church that will limit what others may post on your site, etc.

High tech cannot replace high touch. Technology is simply a means to an end; if we change our focus from what God wants to do in and through us to how we can use the latest and greatest, or to be known as the church with the best toys on the block, then we have allowed the tools to become idols. Let your church be driven by the great commandments and Great Commission more than budgets and technology. Though it may work for the movie, the idea that "if we build it, they will come" does not work for the church. Investing the majority of available finances for the latest gadgets will not draw men and women to Christ.

Invest in quality, and with those who can help you after you get back to your church. More than once did I have to make an emergency call for service on a Sunday morning when something major failed an hour or two before worship services. Saving a few dollars will seem like a poor investment when an emergency arises and the technology is not working or working improperly. Maintain the investments by proper use and by training those who will use them.

BIBLIOGRAPHY

McKeever, Joe. "The Pastor Is the Worship Leader." http://www.churchleaders.com/worship/worship-articles/177026-joe-mckeever-pastor-is-the-worship-leader.html?print.

Readings, Leah. "10 Church Technology Stats that will Astound You." http://blog.capterra.com/church-technology-stats/.

Steele, Ed. *Worship HeartCries: Personal Preparation for Corporate Worship.* Self-published, CreateSpace, 2013.

SECTION 3

Small-Church
Education Ministry

6

Leadership in the Small Church

ADAM HUGHES

I remember well the first time I began to think in a substantial way about the need for, and process of, staffing a small church completely with lay leadership. If any significant and exponential ministry was going to take place in the church I pastored, the work would have to be done by volunteer leaders. It was not that I had never worked with lay leaders previously, nor were any of the biblical truths on the subject of volunteer leadership new or novel to me, it was simply that I had never thought intentionally, nor been forced to think strategically, about what laity as a church's only workforce would look like. All of my previous ministry experience, beginning with my first pastorate, had included other paid ministerial staff, even if only in a bivocational role. This was until I became the pastor of RidgeCrest Baptist Church, a young church plant in Abilene, Texas.

God had called, and in March of 2009 my family and I moved from Fort Worth, Texas, where I was attending seminary, to the west Texas town of Abilene for the purpose of taking over as the first pastor of a modest church plant, which had been in existence for eighteen months without any formal pastoral leadership. My wife and I eagerly approached the task, excited about what God would do with, and among, the fifteen people who constituted the membership of the church. And God did bless us tremendously! It was a sweet and supportive fellowship. Within the first year, we more than doubled in membership and roughly tripled in attendance. We saw several adults profess faith in Christ and follow through in believer's baptism. Thirty-eight members and forty-five to fifty in attendance, however, does not a large church make. And even more to the point, the ministry demands began to expand without the benefit of additional paid staff.

Due to an awareness of this increasing demand, at the culmination of my first year of ministry the two most significant laymen in the church enthusiastically appealed for me to consider what paid staff member I would like to add. They had seen the increase in attendance. They had noticed how God seemed to be blessing. As right as their hearts where, however, they had failed to see reality. Neither our current nor projected budget, even with the increase in attendance, would make the addition of more paid staff a possibility anytime in the foreseeable future.

I began down an important and eye-opening journey concerning leadership in smaller churches then, not as a result of something negative but out of an extremely positive situation. Since I did not want to die from exhaustion in my thirties, I began the process of exploring what the options were for continuing and growing the ministries of our church under the current financial reality. The only possible way forward as a church was to find, train, and empower volunteer leadership within the body for the work of the body. I was forced to think through how this could and would be accomplished. The result was I was led to some principles which are biblical, practical, and sustaining. I had employed some of the practices before, but never in a coalesced, synthesized way for the purpose of developing lay leaders intentionally. I want to share my coalesced and synthesized strategy with you in this chapter.

Before I do, allow me to make two additional statements. The author of this chapter has a deep and longstanding relationship with smaller-membership churches, involvement with smaller church ministry, and thus development of leadership in smaller churches. For instance, over half of my years in pastoral ministry have been spent in churches that average less than 100 in attendance, and practically all of my years in pastoral ministry have been spent pastoring churches that average 250 or less in attendance. This chapter, based on my successes and failures, is designed to help pastors in small-membership churches develop and train leaders. The principles are not only, nor uniquely, true for church plants.

Let me also explain, other than one or two nuances, developing leaders in a smaller-membership church is not greatly different than developing leaders in a larger-membership church. What are these nuances? Motivation and time. In a larger-membership church, a senior pastor can motivate his paid leadership by money or their livelihood. In a smaller-membership church, you do not influence your volunteer lay leadership with financial compensation. Secondly, in a larger-membership church where many, if not all, of your leadership makes their living through ministry, they have more time to go to training because this can be counted as a part of their work hours. Again, this is not usually the case in a smaller-membership church. Other than these considerations, many of the principles listed here for smaller-membership churches would be the same as those for larger-membership churches.

With the above-mentioned points in mind, let us move forward to the subject of lay leadership in the church. As we do so, I will attempt to make a case for the biblical foundation of volunteer leadership in the church, give principles for practically developing volunteer leadership, and give a couple essential tools for the development of volunteer leadership in the church. Remembering that the argument has been made that these principles are biblical, practical, and sustaining, we will attempt to accomplish our task by taking an in-depth look at each of the three parts of this statement. Laypeople trained to do the ministry of the church is biblical. Laypeople trained to do ministry in the church is practical and possible. Laypeople equipped for the ministry of the church is sustaining for the church.

BIBLICAL FOR THE CHURCH

Training laypeople to perform the ministry of the church is biblically valid. At least three closely related truths can be discerned through a study of Scripture regarding the nature of volunteer leaders' involvement in the ministry of the local church.

First, pastors and paid staff members are not commanded, nor assumed, to be responsible for all the work of ministry in the church. In at least one biblical text, the danger of trying to do so can be seen, and the exact opposite exhortation should be applied. Before looking specifically at this aforementioned text, I believe Paul's two lists of the qualifications for the office of pastor in 1 Timothy 3 and Titus 1 are relevant to our discussion. What is missing from these lists is significant. In the list from 1 Timothy 3:1–7, primarily what you see are qualifications related to character. The man of God must be above reproach in all of his dealings and relationships.

Arguably, the only skills that are mentioned are the abilities to teach and to manage his own household aptly so he can, likewise, manage the church.

A similar emphasis is seen in the list from Titus 1:5–9. Again, the thrust of the passage appears to be on the character of the man with the only skill requirement being the ability to apply the word for both the formation of correct doctrine and the correction of false doctrine through his personal commitment to the word of God. A requirement for, or an expectation of, personally doing everything in the body is not in this list. Neither does it seem consistent with what is present in the list. When these lists are examined closely in light of passages like Acts 6 and Ephesians 4:11–16, which we will do below, pastors holding the primary responsibility of doing all the work of ministry in the church is not the focus. As a matter of fact, the exact opposite emphasis seems to arise.

The dangers and impractical nature of such an attempt is seen in the narrative of Exodus 18, a passage of scripture that in administrative circles has become known as the "Jethro Principle."[1] You will remember this text as the passage in which Moses received a visit from his nosey father-in-law, Jethro. The immediate context is that God, through the leadership of Moses, has recently delivered the children of Israel from the oppressive hand of Pharaoh and their enslavement in Egypt. They have not yet taken up residence in the Promised Land. According to what we read immediately afterward in Exodus 19, sometime within the first three months of their departure from Egypt, Jethro came to see the work.

What he found was Moses attempting to personally and comprehensively handle all the daily needs of the Israelites as related to God's word and judgments over their disputes. "It came about the next day that Moses sat to judge the people, and the people stood about Moses from the morning until the evening" (Exod 18:13, NASB). Apparently, by attempting to deal with all the day-to-day minutiae, he had lost his focus on the main call and goal of leading the people of God to take possession of the land. I draw this conclusion because it appears from the text that the task of rendering judgments among people was taking his entire day, and a refocusing on the broader vision of God's plan for Israel is not reengaged until Exodus 19, the chapter after which Jethro counseled Moses. "Now when Moses' father-in-law saw all that he was doing for the people, he said, 'What is this thing you

---

1. For a review of the Exodus 18 passage and a development of the "Jethro Principle," see Welch, *Church Administration*, 1–2.

are doing for the people? Why do you alone sit as judge and all the people stand about you from morning until evening?'" (Exod 18:14, NASB).

Fundamentally, Jethro noticed that this unsustainable practice was wearing Moses out, as well as the people. "Moses' father-in-law said to him, 'The thing that you are doing is not good. You will surely wear out, both yourself and these people who are with you, for the task is too heavy for you; you cannot do it alone'" (Exod 18:17–18, NASB). So Jethro offered Moses a very wise and concrete solution. Jethro's counsel was for Moses to only handle the major issues, but appoint other men under him who would hold authority over the minor disputes and inquiries of the people in iterations of thousands, hundreds, fifties, and tens.

> Furthermore, you shall select out of all the people able men who fear God, men of truth, those who hate dishonest gain; and you shall place *these* over them as leaders of thousands, of hundreds, of fifties, and of tens. Let them judge the people at all times; and let it be that every major dispute they will bring to you, but every minor dispute they themselves will judge (Exod 18:21–22a, NASB).

The solution, if applied rightly, would be a blessing to both Moses and the people. "If you do this thing and God so commands you, then you will be able to endure, and all these people also will go to their place in peace" (Exod 18:23, NASB). Implied in this statement perhaps is that the solution applied will be a double blessing for the people because they still get their daily needs met and gain back their leader's focus on the primary task which God has given him. And a blessing for Moses will result because he will have help in the daily tasks and gain back the freedom to focus on the primary mission for which God had called him.

What does this text communicate about the biblical nature of lay leadership in the church generally, and the scriptural precedent that pastors are not called, nor expected, to do all the work in the church specifically? At this point, the answer to these questions may be obvious but allow me to be explicit. Our major concern here is not the implementation in the church of the specific plan that Jethro gave Moses, only what the need for the existence of that plan may say about pastors and the church. Acknowledging the passage is not talking directly about church ministry or to a pastor, I believe a fair implication may be made for our subject under consideration.

The connection between a pastor's calling and lay leadership's responsibility in a church, and that which we see in Exodus 18, is situated in Moses' role as God's man chosen as the primary leader of God's community of faith. Israel was designated as the people of God and Moses had attempted and failed to effectively serve the people's needs alone.

The text is clear that Moses was God's chosen leader and mouthpiece for his people. "Now listen to me: I will give you counsel, and God be with you. You be the people's representative before God, and you bring the disputes to God, then teach them the statutes and the laws, and make known to them the way in which they are to walk and the work they are to do" (Exod 18:19–20, NASB). Also, we see from the context of the Pentateuch as a whole, and Exodus uniquely, that Israel is God's Old Testament community of faith. In a similar, although not exact, way that Moses was leading God's people, the pastor is called to lead the church. Whereas it was impossible for one person to do all the work of leading Israel well, one person, even in a smaller-membership situation, cannot do all the work of leading a church well. Finally, as can be deduced from the text, even though specific qualifications where made of them, none of the men who Moses was to select to help him do the work were of necessity from the lineage that would become the Aaronic priesthood or the Levites. The absence of an indication in the text that those who were appointed to serve were professional, or those called or consecrated by God in a unique way, is significant. All of the above-mentioned gives credence to the position that it is not a biblical command or intention, nor is it practical for a pastor to be responsible for all of the work of the ministry of the church. Laity can and should be involved in the work and service of the community of faith!

Second, volunteer leaders, including the office or role of deacon, are included in the practice of the ministry of the church. Two passages are noteworthy here. Of the two passages under consideration, one may be more recognizable than the other. The first text is Acts 6:1–7. This is a well-known passage in which laymen are employed for the hands-on service of the church. The context is that some time after the ascension of Christ, Pentecost, and the birth and explosion of the New Testament Church in Jerusalem, a problem arose among the membership. The foreign-born Jewish widows were feeling neglected or underserved in the daily distribution of food. So, the short story is the church leadership and the body agreed to appoint seven men who would take up the responsibility of this ministry.

Space does not allow us to fully examine all of the nuances of this passage, but a few conclusions can be drawn. First, even though there is some debate in scholarship as to whether or not this is the genesis of the office of deacon, we can say with certainty that we see an example here of laity being used in the leadership and the practice of ministry in the church. Second, even though we should not make a one-to-one comparison between apostles and pastors, we can understand from this passage that the point of this solution was to free up the uniquely equipped leaders in the church to focus on the bigger picture to which God had called them. Finally, the result of the implementation for the church here is noteworthy. "The word of God kept on spreading; and the number of the disciples continued to increase greatly in Jerusalem, and a great many of the priests were becoming obedient to the faith" (Acts 6:7, NASB).

A lesser-known text which deals with the laity's involvement in the work of the mission of the church is Titus 2:1–8. Again, space will not allow us a full examination of the passage, but a biblical foundation for the responsibility of volunteers in the church can be inferred, if not explicated, from a few of the details of the text. In this passage, you have a command from Paul to Titus, a pastor of the church in Crete, to instruct his members to be involved in the discipleship ministry, or ministry of the word, of the church. He calls for older ladies in the church, by the word and for the sake of the reputation of the word, to disciple younger ladies in the church:

> Older women likewise are to be reverent in their behavior, not malicious gossips nor enslaved to much wine, teaching what is good, so that they may encourage the young women to love their husbands, to love their children, to be sensible, pure, workers at home, kind, being subject to their own husbands, so that the word of God will not be dishonored" (Titus 2:3–5, NASB).

A similar call seems to exist for the men of the church as well.

> Older men are to be temperate, dignified, sensible, sound in faith, in love, in perseverance. . . . Likewise urge the young men to be sensible; in all things show yourself to be an example of good deeds, with purity in doctrine, dignified, sound in speech which is beyond reproach, so that the opponent will be put to shame, having nothing bad to say about us" (Titus 2:2, 6–8, NASB).

At a minimum, we see in the text of Titus 2 that the responsibility for the discipleship ministry, instruction in and responsibility for the church, and reputation of the gospel extends beyond the pastor. The New Testament affirms the role of lay leadership in the work and responsibility of ministry in the church.

Finally, the New Testament testifies that pastors explicitly are to have the responsibility of including and equipping church members for the work of ministry. This aforementioned truth is displayed in Ephesians 4:11–16. In verses 13 through 16, the nuances of the body being the body are many and the application for the church is rich, but for our purposes let's focus for a moment on verses 11 and 12. "And He gave some as apostles, and some as prophets, and some as evangelists, and some as pastors and teachers, for the equipping of the saints for the work of service, to the building up of the body of Christ;. . . . " At least three details are paramount in the passage concerning the case that church members are to be trained to do the work of the ministry of the church.

First, the designation "saints" in the passage does not refer to the spiritually elite or a professional class of Christians. In the Greek language, the designation is literally "holy ones," meaning all those whom Christ has saved and made holy. The passage is referring to the regular church members.

Second, the regular church member here is to be equipped for the work of service, or ministry in the church, implying then that he or she should indeed do this work so the whole church receives a benefit. Notice, concerning the end result or purpose of such work, Paul wrote, "to the building up of the body of Christ."

Finally, according to this text, a primary reason pastors, staff, and ministers are called and given to the church is not so they would do everything in and for the church, but for the purpose and result that the regular church member be equipped to do the work of the ministry of the church. "And He gave some as apostles, and some as prophets, and some as evangelists, and some as pastors and teachers, *for the equipping of the saints* for the work of service,. . . . "(Emphasis added). Therefore, two safe and related conclusions may be made. First, the equipping and empowering of lay leadership by pastors and congregations in the local church for the work of ministry is biblical. And second, biblical leadership must involve volunteer lay leadership.

So far in this chapter, we have looked at the biblical position of, and the theological support for, volunteers being used in the leadership and practice of the ministry in the church. I hope this review of Scripture has convinced both you as a pastor and subsequently the church you lead of the theological impetus of this practice. But even if it has, you may be wondering how do I effectively accomplish the training and use of laity in the leadership of the church. The next section gives some practical and hopefully time-efficient how-to's for developing lay leaders in the smaller-church ministry setting.

PRACTICAL PRINCIPLES FOR THE CHURCH

Training laypeople to lead ministry is practical for, and possible in, the church. Below I will list six principles for equipping leaders in a small-church setting. I have intentionally referred to these as principles here instead of steps. The reason for the nomenclature "principles" instead of "steps" is two-fold. First, they are not listed in chronological order. Other than the first principle, the order is not the priority. One does not necessarily build on the other. Second, the list does not constitute a process to be completed but an ongoing strategy to be employed. The point is not getting to the end of the process. The point, rather, is that these principles should be continual in your strategy as a leader and continuous in the life of those you are equipping to be leaders. In that way, the development of leaders, or of even one individual leader, is never a completed process. After listing the principles, I will conclude by describing a few resources that may be helpful in your process.

First, place prospective volunteer leaders in a position to succeed from the beginning. In other words, invite them to participate in areas for which they have already shown an interest or displayed an aptitude. If you are like me, you have seen or even caused a scenario similar to what follows. You are meeting with the nominating committee picking leaders and teachers for the next church year. You are having trouble filling the last one or two spots on the finance team and finding a teacher for that class no one wants to teach. So, you pull out the church roll and begin to list several people until you arrive at a couple names which grabs everyone's attention. The best, and perhaps only, qualification for these people is that you think you can get them to say yes. They rarely say no to anything. So you approach Bob about serving on the finance team, even though everyone knows that his personal finances are a mess, and Linda about teaching the ladies' class, even though she is so shy she struggles to sing aloud in worship. And, best of all you tell them, "It's easy, doesn't take a lot of commitment, and anyone can do it." Now, God may very well have called Bob to trust Christ more with his personal finances so he can aid the church's finances. Linda may need more faith that God will give her all she needs to be used by him in a teaching role. However, neither of these commitments are easy, and they do take a lot of time. Worse still, not everyone should serve on the finance team and certainly not everyone can and should teach!

If your goal is to cause someone to fail miserably, never serve again, and possibly leave your church, then by all means follow the pattern that was listed above. However, if your goal is to see someone used in the church, serve with joy, and succeed in leadership, put him or her in a ministry they have a passion for, and gifting in. Case in point, I had a deacon in the second church I pastored whom I will call Larry, and he seemed to have a heart and gifting for caring for widows and shut-ins. I saw this in display almost every Tuesday morning when voluntarily he would show up, make copies of the previous Sunday's sermon, and hand-deliver these copies to every shut-in senior lady who had expressed an interest in having one. He would even set the tape to the appropriate starting point in a tape player, so all they had to do to listen was push play (Yes, this was back when people still used tape players.). It made sense to me that both Larry and the church body would be blessed if I found a way to get him more involved with, and in leadership of, the ministry of caring for our seniors. This is exactly what we did as a church. My encouragement regarding lay leaders is to first see where their interests lie and match them up to and develop their gifts for that type of ministry.

Second, spend significant amounts of time with the prospective and current volunteer leaders in your church. There are at least two reasons to do so. First, knowing someone's interests and gifting would be difficult if not impossible if you were never around them. As I began to notice Larry's heart for widows and shut-ins, I looked for opportunities to observe him more closely before I ever talked with him about expanding his role and scope of influence. On more than one occasion, I would ride with him as he delivered the tapes of Sunday's sermon and notice how he conducted himself toward these precious members of our congregation. His genuine care was palpable.

Now, I will acknowledge that the practice of riding with Larry took precious time away from other important parts of my ministry and was a significant commitment on my part. From my perspective, however, doing so was essential because, during these times, I was allowed to see his passion first-hand. I believe God confirmed and developed in me a vision for his leadership in the area of senior adult and widow ministry in our church by observing Larry in action and in his element.

In regard to spending significant amounts of time with those God may be calling to be leaders in the church, I also am reminded of two young men—whom I will call Chris and Nick—who were both students and members of the church plant in Abilene. Both had a passion for the church and had expressed a call to ministry or leadership in the church. Nick seemed to have a gifting in music whereas Chris had a love for teenagers and teaching the Bible in general. I began the practice of meeting with both of them early on Tuesday mornings at a local Subway. I led them through a study of portions of the Pastoral Epistles, but I mainly answered their questions and became a resource to them. I certainly got to know them, their giftings, and their hearts, but they also got to know me, my passion, and my heart. Not only do you need to get to know your leadership, but your leadership must have access to you so they get to know and trust you. A second benefit, therefore, of spending significant amounts of time with leaders and potential leaders in your church is mutual trust and access.

Third, model ministry for them. If we desire as pastors to be effective in forming and training lay leaders, we must do more than tell them what to do. They must see us in action. We must set the example for them. This goes hand-in-hand with spending significant amounts of time with the prospective and current volunteer leaders in your church. Learn to marry the concepts of modeling ministry for them with every opportunity that you have to be with them. And, look for opportunities to be with them so you can model ministry for them.

Going back to the example of Larry, after observing him in action and seeing his heart for the widows and shut-ins in our church, I strategically began to invite him to go with me when I engaged in ministry to senior adults and widows. For instance, when I was going to visit someone in the hospital who fit into this demographic, I would call Larry to accompany me. If I had a nursing home visit to make, I would see if Larry was available. I wanted him to see how I cared for people in these situations. I wanted him to observe how I spoke to them, what questions I asked, how I comforted them with Scripture, and how I prayed for and over them. I wanted to present a living model of ministry for him.

In a similar way, I liked to, whenever possible, take a church member with me on guest follow-up and evangelism visitation. I try to do the same thing in door-to-door evangelism with students at the seminary, as do several other faculty members. I especially like to have someone with me who has rarely or never personally shared the gospel. I want them to observe how I begin a conversation, notice how I transition to spiritual matters, and hear exactly how I share the gospel. My desire has always been to allow them to be with me so I can serve as a living model for personal evangelism. Setting an example in and for ministry is part of the reason why it is so important for you to spend time with your potential leaders. Let them see you doing what you are going to ask them to do.

Fourth, frequently give them times of informal training. The principle of informal training essentially is a synthesis of the previous two. The most effective training, and certainly the most effective training for which a lay leader has time, can often be accomplished in modeling ministry for them as you are spending significant amounts of time together. This practice may be called the pedagogy of imitation. By this I mean the method of teaching (pedagogy) in which the skill or practice is acquired by the student seeing and repeating (imitation) what the teacher or mentor does. This method is a thoroughly biblical concept (i.e., Jesus with his disciples and Paul with Timothy). This method is a thoroughly practical concept. Think about it: most of the functional things you do in life such as walk, talk, and eat, you learned to some degree through imitation. From the perspective of the pastor, the call here is to make sure you are being intentional about what skills you are attempting to teach your mentee. Have a plan!

Fifth, find occasional formal training sessions for the prospective and volunteer leaders in your church. A great possibility for formal in-house training is a sermon series on 1 Timothy, Titus, or Ephesians 4 in which general principles about the church, a leader's calling, a leader's qualifications, and a leader's responsibility to the church are highlighted. The series could be accompanied with a study guide or study questions that you later use in a meeting with those you are equipping for ministry. Strengths of this possibility include the need for minimal extra time on the part of the volunteer (they presumably are already listening to the sermon) and the call for minimal extra work on the part of the pastor (you presumably are already preparing sermons and preaching on a regular basis). Some questions for discussion could be developed while preparing the application portion of your message, and the questions could be discussed at an hour-long meeting before Wednesday night activities.

A few other options for formal training include soliciting the help of your local Baptist association, your Baptist state convention, or a larger sister church with which you develop a relationship. In every church I have pastored, I have taken church members to one-day associational workshops and Vacation Bible School sessions and had state convention employees come to us for children's worker and adult Sunday school training. One specific training event I scheduled involved my time at the church plant in Abilene. Our sponsor church was a large congregation in Lubbock, Texas.

They had a full complement of ministries with well-trained and paid staff coordinating most of them. One Sunday night, approximately ten to fifteen of their staff and lay leaders came to us. They broke us up into several specific areas of ministry, which we were trying to develop and staff. Then, they gave us instruction and training in these specific areas of ministry. They concluded the night by answering any questions we had, and they gave our volunteer leaders their contact information with the invitation to call any time they could be a resource. This may have been the most successful lay leader training session of which I have been a part. I believe this was the case for a few reasons. It was cheap, it required no travel, it was conducted in our ministry context, and it was conducted by practitioners who were currently in a church doing it successfully.

The details and success of this training session does lead to a couple of general cautions to be observed regardless of what formal training you choose for your leaderships. Make sure it is inexpensive. Make the training sessions no longer than one-day events when possible. Keep them in as close proximity to your church as you can. And, make sure they are worth the time.

Finally, both formalizing the new volunteer leaders' roles in the church and celebrating their accomplishments in ministry are great ideas. You need to let them, and the entire congregation, know you trust them to do what they have been trained for and encourage them to take the responsibility to do it. The last situation you want to develop after you have done all of the work of identifying, investing in, and encouraging new leaders is for them to never get off the runway. You want to support them, hold them accountable, and continue to be a resource for them, but you do not want to continue to do all of the ministry yourself. This pattern would be counterproductive at best. You also want to make sure you recognize the work, success, and accomplishments of your volunteer leaders in their ministry and before the church. Both formalizing the new volunteer's role and celebrating his or her accomplishments can be as simple as a prayer in a worship gathering or as elaborate as an end-of-the-year banquet.

Allow me to end this section by pointing you to three helpful tools. First, I would encourage you to pick up Aubrey Malphurs's book *Being Leaders: The Nature of Authentic Christian Leadership.*[2] Even though it is a little dated, this book is a helpful resource for the discipline of pastoral leadership. I would direct you specifically to chapter 8, "A Directional Leader: The Leader's Task," in which he offers guidance for helping follow-

2. Malphurs, *Being Leaders: The Nature of Authentic Christian Leadership.*

ers develop a personal ministry mission and a personal vision statement.[3] The information contained in this discussion is invaluable for helping volunteer leadership understand and focus on precisely what God is calling them to accomplish with their lives. Second, Robert Welch's work, *Church Administration: Creating Efficiency for Effective Ministry*, is a thorough, substantial work in the area of church administration.[4] As mentioned above, I believe for the purposes of our discussion you will find his unpacking of the "Jethro Principle" uniquely helpful.[5] The two works listed here are the primary texts we use in our Master's degree course, "Church Leadership and Administration," at New Orleans Baptist Theological Seminary.

The final tool I will draw your attention to is relationships. Develop relationships! Here, I am not only talking about relationships with your lay leaders. I am also talking about relationships with Baptist associations, state conventions, and other pastors and churches in your area. Call your association and state convention. They work for you and will be quick to tell you so. Other pastors and churches, especially larger ones, may have resources and training they are willing to share with you. They may keep you from having to reinvent the wheel in your ministry. You will never know, however, if you do not develop relationships with them. Relationships, therefore, are an essential tool for developing the laity into the leaders of the ministry in your church.

SUSTAINING FOR THE CHURCH

Basically two schools of thought exist for staffing ministries in the church. The first is to hire the professionals to do all the work. In this model, hired and paid ministers lead all of the areas of ministry in the church. Volunteer laymen may be used but only in a secondary capacity. Larger churches or churches with larger budgets typically follow this practice. The second is to use the average church member to be the leadership and the workforce of the ministries of the church. Most smaller-membership churches by necessity follow some derivative of this model. The problem is they usually do it without intentionality at best, or poorly at worst. What I have done in this chapter is attempt to describe some principles for helping you employ the latter model successfully.

3. Ibid., 157–72.
4. Welch, *Church Administration: Creating Efficiency for Effective Ministry*.
5. Ibid., 1–2.

I am convinced this model is the best practice for two reasons, even if you are a large church or a small church that will eventually hire part-time or full-time staff. First, even if you hire staff, if you have taken the time and have a pattern of equipping volunteer leaders well in certain areas of ministry, then when new staff is hired they already have a well-trained workforce. They will benefit greatly from this practice. Second, staff members and pastors come and go, but if you have a well-trained volunteer workforce, they will be able to sustain and grow the ministry during times of transition. This model also keeps ministry consistent for the church over longer periods of time. Therefore, in either small or larger churches, the practice of equipping and employing volunteers to lead and staff ministries is more sustaining for the church in the long-run.

CONCLUSION

Candidly, I did not get to see these principles come to fruition in RidgeCrest. Maybe poor execution on my part or simply God's timing was the reason. I began the process and was seeing some progress, but I did not get to finish the plan. God called us to another place of ministry. Maybe in your current ministry setting or one for which God is preparing you, you will be able to begin, complete, and see the fruits of this process for developing and using volunteer leaders in the ministry of the local church. In smaller-membership churches, leadership is an interesting mix of pastor, family, and congregation. As challenging as it may be at times, and even if you modify the process somewhat, allow me to encourage you to continue the work. These principles are biblical, practical, and sustaining. Laypeople trained to do the ministry of the church is biblical. Laypeople trained to do ministry in the church is practical and possible. Laypeople equipped for the ministry of the church is sustaining for the church. God bless you as you develop and empower laymen and women to the task of ministry leadership in the local church.

BIBLIOGRAPHY

Malphurs, Aubrey. *Being Leaders: The Nature of Authentic Christian Leadership.* Grand Rapids: Baker, 2003.

Welch, Robert H. *Church Administration: Creating Efficiency for Effective Ministry,* 2nd ed. Nashville: B&H Academic, 2001.

7

Church Administration in the Small Church

Jody Dean

S maller-membership churches may not have considered many areas of church administration because they believe some of the issues only deal with the churches that have a larger facility, more programs, and more people. This chapter is written to provide information on church administration for the smaller-membership church. The cultural shift toward a litigious environment does not consider the size of a congregation. In the following sections you will be led to consider the various components of church administration in which smaller-membership churches and ministers should garner an understanding to lead effectively in the administrative areas of the church. We begin by considering the guiding documents that any church has to have and some that should be created. These documents should be your framework for leading, providing governance, and creating teams to accomplish the ministry of your church. The finances of the ministry—from receiving tithes and offerings and accounting for expenses, to considerations for fundraising issues and designated giving—will be considered. Other considerations will be leadership qualifications and accountability for paid staff and volunteers as well as legal considerations.

In many communities, the safety and protection of the people gathered in the church, as well as the property and facilities, has become a concern. People need to feel safe when they are part of your congregation.

The security considerations for creating a plan to protect your people will already be provided. Church facilities need to have some components that will help you in your ministry as you teach and make disciples. These are simple considerations for classrooms, restrooms, and people with special access needs. These facilities considerations extend to your transportation as well. If you utilize personally owned vehicles for the church or own vehicles yourself, then you will need to consider transportation concerns in our litigious society.

The last area of concern will be creating a pathway for vetting your people before they serve in ministry with minors. The insurance provider for your church will need to be consulted for several areas that will be mentioned to determine if you have coverage, need additional coverage, or are already covered. My prayer for you as you read this chapter is that the information will serve to guide you and provide a resource in considering what you can do to be more effective in these litigious areas that could impact you and the church you serve.

GUIDING DOCUMENTS

A few guiding documents should exist in any size congregation. The first of those key documents is the church's constitution and bylaws. The constitution should state the name of the church and the physical location of the church. Doctrinal statements should address the following: basic beliefs, dogma, and polity. Membership qualifications and how they accomplish their cooperative work as a body are necessary as well. Bylaws should address the rights and privileges of the members, responsibilities and powers of church officers, process for becoming a church officer, and how long one will serve as an officer. In addition, the bylaws should include the rules for executing business and conducting meetings, who the moderator for the meetings will be, and what constitutes a quorum (the official number of membership needed for an official business meeting). A minister should know the content of these documents when leading a congregation.

The minister and key leaders should research whether or not the guiding documents in use are the official documents of the church. Sometimes the paper trail for documents cannot be confirmed and thus the older documents of record are still the official guiding documents for the congregation. Different states have unique caveats to their laws, and the church should be sure their guiding documents are in compliance. Although the church may have members that assume a standard for operating the church exists based on historical practices, the documents should outline how they were installed, how they can be officially modified, and how the assets are distributed if the organization ceases to exist.[1] Many churches have existed for decades and the manner for conducting the business of the church has morphed over time as both the membership and the ministers on staff have changed. The paper trail for the documents needs to be verified. If the validity of the documents for your church is questionable, then—with the leadership—navigate a pathway to confirm legal guiding documents for your church.

Incorporation is a step with the state that validates your existence as a chartered-nonprofit religious organization. Due to the changing times in American society, churches should consider their incorporation status. You may be incorporated due to the affiliation with an association or the state convention, but many churches have chosen to incorporate in addition to their affiliations. "All states and territories of the United States have provisions for nonprofit organizations to incorporate as a corporate entity, enjoying the privileges—as well as the responsibilities—that any corporation may have."[2] Each state has a specific application process that varies from state to state for filing for incorporation. Most require a filed application that outlines the institution, physical location, officers, and incorporators. You will also be charged a fee to file and be required to prove you are operating as a chartered-nonprofit, religious organization. This can be evidenced in some states with copies of official church constitution and bylaws, and in some states the Internal Revenue Code 501(c)(3) tax-exempt registration is required. Although this process for incorporation may seem exhaustive and difficult, it should be considered for the benefit of the congregation to formalize their existence in another official manner.[3]

Another document your church should consider having in place is a policy and procedure manual. You create policies for the routine functions and operations of your church. Examples would be the facility use policy for groups that are not a part of your church. In addition, guidelines for weddings, transportation, fundraisers, and the church office are a few examples of general policies a church may routinely encounter. Policy should be used to outline the responses for routine operations of the church. Procedures

1. Welch, *Church Administration*, 52.
2. Ibid., 55.
3. Ibid., 55.

then explain how to carry out the general policy. The guidelines for a wedding at your church, the van use guidelines, guidelines for what types of fundraisers, and guidelines for office hours are examples of procedures that accompany policy. During a business meeting the church membership should approve your policy and procedure manual and any changes that merit a church vote. Many policies and procedures can be amended or added by your key committees for building, finance, and personnel since most policies and procedures will deal with those key areas of ministry.

LEADING THE PEOPLE AND GOVERNANCE

Leading a team-based ministry in a smaller church deals with ministry execution, Sunday school, and age-grade ministry. Committees are a great way to address key governing and management issues in the church. A building committee that addresses the facility needs for maintenance and oversight of the property is a key committee to accomplish the mission. Finance is another committee that provides oversight for the budget and overall stewardship of resources to fund the vision and mission that the congregation sets out to accomplish. A personnel committee for a smaller church can involve more people than first imagined and be influential in staffing the church to accomplish the mission. These three committees deal with the major components of business in the church as each church has a facility to manage or share, a budget to manage, and a staff to take care of the ministry. Many ministers who are bivocational are thankful for a group of people who manage the problems with the facility and keep the grounds in a presentable manner for each service. You should try to teach this leadership team that their role is servant leadership to manage and care for the facility and not boss or control the facility. The finance committee can be a great resource for the church if they are led by a ministry direction and not just spending and saving. The personnel team can be a great encouragement if they understand their role is to provide accountability and not to control the work of ministry. Many churches have some support staff from part-time office or custodial assistance. In addition, ministerial staff may help direct music and/or youth ministries with a pastor on staff. A personnel committee can be crucial in providing oversight for human resources when many, if not all, of the church staff are part-time and volunteer.

Although your church may have more than three committees to oversee the administrative work of the church that covers transportation, insurance, and security, the focus should move away from committees to ministry teams to accomplish the work of the church.

Missions, bereavement, benevolence, women, children, and youth are all ministries that could have a committee or a ministry team for leading in that area of focus. I believe people are open to be equipped for ministry more on a team than serving as a member of a committee. A committee communicates an expectation to govern, whereas a ministry team communicates a collective group equipping others to serve in an area of ministry. The concept of a team is an administrative approach to providing a hands-on group of leaders to accomplish the work of a specific ministry. For instance, the children's ministry does not need a committee of people who are not currently serving in that ministry. A committee should consist of those already serving, who can help decide how to lead and execute that area of ministry. I believe people would prefer to be coached as a team and work together to accomplish ministry. Think back over your life and determine if a coach with a team was more effective for you or a business-style committee. To effectively lead a team-based ministry, leadership development and disciple-making take time; but when implemented together, the results are incredible. I suggest you find three people you can coach for three key areas of ministry focus. You do not want to get overwhelmed and it will be a challenge to accomplish everything, which is why taking a strategic focus can be rewarding as you impact ministry through serving as the head coach. In addition, you will have your three key committee chairman as well as one chairman of deacons to make a strategic investment into their lives.

You now have seven key relationships as a small-church leader that need to be cultivated. This many people may be more than you can handle, so you need to find a person you can trust to share the load of coaching. Many leaders suggest having only five direct reports that you cultivate. You will have to determine your key relationships, leaders, and focus for your time to coach the people you lead well. Many times as leaders we struggle to be like Moses managing all the people and not leading a few key people well in the process.

You may be familiar with the concept of having the right people on your leadership bus; however, you need them on the bus and in the right seat for everything to work as designed. In the book, *Good to Great* by Jim Collins, the concept of having the right people functioning in the right roles on your leadership bus is key to success.[4] In a church sometimes we have people in positions based on their years of involvement at the church, family connection, or simply their availability to fill a position. The guiding documents should help you establish criteria for your key leadership positions. You need qualifications for leaders in your church that can make key decisions as outlined in your bylaws, but you also need qualifications for leaders in the church that hold specific offices. A deacon, Bible teacher, or volunteer with minors should all be vetted for scriptural qualifications to be installed in their positions. Accountability can be hard in the smaller church where everyone is close in relationship, much like a family. You do not want to create a family feud, but you do need to be sure the ministry is not discredited because a leader's life in the home and community does not comply with his position in the church.

Safeguarding the work of the church through members using their gifts can be a challenge. Many people have indwelling issues in their lives that may not surface in public. As leaders we have to be sure we have background checks to vet our leaders and volunteers in all ministries. In addition, we need to have a process where we meet with potential volunteers and talk about their conversion, baptism, church membership, and walk with Christ. I would also encourage you to consider the social media profile of a leader. Many churches have adopted a social media policy to help leaders understand the importance of public and online representation. Your smaller-membership church may not have a website and social interaction may be limited, but in a society where people are constantly connected you should safeguard your ministry from internet dangers as much as possible. Ministry cannot be accomplished without volunteers, yet you may struggle to staff each area and are afraid that taking these steps may cause that problem to increase. While those concerns are valid, it is important to protect the ministry by having qualified leaders in place for the ministry of your church.

PROTECTING THE PEOPLE AND PROPERTY

Violence and misconduct involving churches in the twenty-first century has caused many of us to be shocked, discouraged, or afraid due to the number of incidents involving church members or outside threats to the church property or people that are a part of the church. The reality of arson,

4. Collins, *Good to Great*, 41.

an active shooter during a service, a person having a medical episode during service, robbery, and inappropriate adult behavior with a minor area are a few areas of safety and security any church should consider in their weekly schedule and special events. While I pray these issues never surface in your congregation, unfortunately one or more of these issues occur in a church each week. A few considerations will be given for your church to help you start the journey of safety and security for your church. In your preschool and children's area, do you allow anyone to walk in those areas each week? You should consider creating a safer environment by only allowing parents or guardians and workers in those areas. Consider the outdoor parking lot and perimeter at night time for potential threats as people leave the property. Sometimes we use residential and not commercial equipment in the preschool/children's space, and you should consider the safety of those items. Be sure cribs and diaper-changing stations are safe and secure during the times they are in use. Food allergies are a concern the church should consider when feeding snacks or meals with preschool, children, and youth.

Every threat or possibility cannot be addressed, but being as safe as your church can be and offering as secure an environment as possible is the highest level a shepherd can take in protecting the flock from harm. A shepherd knows the major threats and those that are most frequent to his herd and thus provides the appropriate protection needed. You should be aware of the potential for crime in your community. If burglary is on the rise, then you may need a security system. If your area has had several weeks of suspicious activity, you may need a security team to take a rotation of walking around with a heightened sensitivity to outside threats. This topic ranges from theft or destruction of property to harming of people. The church building was once regarded with a higher level of respect; however, today we live in a time when people are selfish and will do whatever they feel is needed to fuel their addiction or position. In addition, we have increased numbers of people that are not in agreement with the Christian church and desire to cause her or the Christians that make up the church harm. Consider the cluttered hallways, overcrowded closets, and doorways, and provide a safer environment in the classrooms and worship center as people gather each week. We sometimes forget about looking for potential hazards since we are there on a weekly basis. Also consider ways to secure your age-graded ministry each week. You may have to increase lighting in your parking lot, limit entry points to your building, or install security cameras as ways to enhance your security. Jesus made it a point in his teaching for us to be reminded to diligently care for the children and be sure they did not stumble. Your church may not be able to provide everything, but you can find ways to become safer and more secure in your ministry.

FINANCES OF THE CHURCH

Another area of church administration that can be a stumbling block is finances. Money can be a hot topic in ministry that creates a wealth of emotion. The finances of the church should be a discipleship component. Tithing is a commitment to the Lord to give back as he has freely given. Safeguarding the finances of the church is a component of stewardship that should be considered. A few issues that need to be addressed in any church are how money is received, recorded, and deposited. Once money is given, what is your process to then record the donation and the information needed, and then deposit the funds into the church's account at the bank? This would be a good time also to consider designated giving. Some churches have a list of numerous designated funds in addition to the general operating account. A consideration that can make a difference is to limit the number of designated accounts in your church. The general fund, building fund, and missions are three designated accounts that are common. Many churches choose to add more designated accounts for each ministry or project a member names or decides to give toward. Stewardship of these funds can be a challenge when you let somebody with a few dollars give and create a fund that may or may not accomplish the church's goals. In addition, designated funds for specific projects without church approval and involvement may never receive enough money to be accomplished and then remain in the account never to be utilized. A designated account and giving policy that determines a process for the church to establish and manage new designated accounts may be a challenge but is needed in every church. This will establish a pathway for dealing with a church member's pet project that may or may not fit with the entire congregations' desire before a check is written and a designated account then created.

Accounting procedures with checks and balances are crucial for a church. I have heard it stated many times no one would ever steal from the church. However, I have seen people take sleeves of cups and plates thinking that because they tithe they are entitled. Although this scenario is not money, it does take away resources for ministry. Another scenario could be a twenty-dollar bill each week slipped into a pocket while one usher counts loose plate (any cash and change not in an envelope). A twenty-dollar bill each week at 52 weeks equals $1,040 per year. If he counts loose plate for twenty years, then his bring-home, tax-free loose plate tip has now totaled $20,800. A little misuse here and there in any church can equal large sums of money that costs ministry for years to come. A simple procedure would be to never let money be counted or handled alone. Rotate the people so the same two are not always counting the money. Create a purchasing policy and procedure so people are not spending money without first acquiring permission to do so.

What type of budget does your church utilize each year? Some people develop a budget based on dreams instead of reality and will place unrealistic numbers to categories. Then they struggle to fund the work because they overestimated the income. Many families operate their household budget in this manner and thus enter into debt just to pay for last month's lifestyle. A church has to be sure the budget and income are realistic for their size, and live within their operating means. I also suggest a three-month operating cushion in reserve for the hard times or unexpected events. If you live in an area where you could miss a few weeks of offering due to hurricane evacuations, or with snow that causes a couple of Sunday cancellations per year, then you need to consider these issues with your reserve fund balance within your operating account. Although you can find many recommendations for best practices concerning church finances, you need to trust the Lord to provide for the work in the church. I have witnessed a difficult budget year wrought with unexpected expenses and seen the Lord provide through unique and unforeseen people and events.

An external audit may be worth the investment every couple of years if you cannot afford an outside audit each year. The benefit of someone looking at your expenses and income from the outside will be to improve accountability and trust people will have for the accounting of tithes and offerings. If we challenge our people to be good stewards of their resources, then an external audit reveals that we are corporately striving to be good stewards. You should also consider an accounting software system that can utilized for records. I know some churches still utilize hand-written checks and an excel file to track the budget. Although this is workable, a computer software program for accounting that can be backed up and print checks can limit fraudulent practices. The bottom line for finances in the church is to have a system for recording contributions, create a purchasing requisition process, and ensure that your church is being a good steward of the resources given through the congregation. A personal note in regard to finances is my experience with the Cooperative Program. I grew up in an SBC church that instilled the value of tithing to the Cooperative Program for the collective mission work around the world through the SBC. I have never forgotten that lesson and encourage you and your church to consider a strong commitment to the Cooperative Program through your church budget.

FACILITY AND PROPERTY CONCERNS

Insurance, utilities, and maintenance are fixed aspects of the church budget that provide a facility for your church to gather and accomplish ministry in a specific geographical context. A clean facility that is in good working order is a crucial component to creating an environment for ministry to occur. Any given year a facility will have issues from mechanical, normal wear and tear, and systematic repairs to keep major issues at bay. Facilities can consume a smaller budget when major repairs occur because facility issues were not forecasted to help the church prepare and plan to take care of their needs.

Although maintenance can be a major issue, another consideration should be the first impression of the property when a person arrives from the parking lot to the first hello inside the building. Directional signage can help a first-time guest know where to enter the building and how to navigate your space from the fellowship hall to classrooms or to the preschool area to leave a baby. A facility that is older may not have considered the design of classrooms or the furnishings of that space. I do not subscribe to the latest and greatest when addressing facilities, but I do believe safe, clean, and well-cared-for space is a bottom line for most families. If you do not agree, when is the last time you passed on a fast food restaurant for cleanliness, resolved to never stop at that gas station again, or thought Wal-Mart could be better prepared for your shopping experience? The reality for the church is our space in American society matters for these reasons. The church should desire to have facilities that do not appear to be a generation removed and irrelevant for people today.

Church building design in previous years did not always consider the issue of visibility in ministry areas with minors. Each classroom should have a window within the door. Simple steps to facility maintenance can range from stretching carpet that is a tripping hazard because of wrinkling with age, updating the look by replacing dated furnishings in entrances, or new landscaping and brighter lighting for the parking lot. Another concern in an aging facility is paint, which can be addressed in a few work days. Fresh paint will create a better smell and look to your space. Many churches have stairs, and you should consider handicap ramps and bathrooms for your church as well as the tread on the stairs for safety.

VOLUNTEERS AND MINORS

Minors should be with two adults that are not related in a classroom. You should have worker screening and training that demonstrates your best effort to provide minors a physically, mentally, emotionally, and spiritually growing environment. Churches have precious children under their care who should be given the best from your people and space. Your church does not have to look like the ministries of another church, but should create a loving and nurturing environment that meets their needs. A consistent team of adults who provides a quality ministry is a great way to reach families. Parents expect a ministry to care for and nurture—not harm— their children. They are concerned with the people that will minister to their child. Background checks and protective measures are now minimal standards for ministry with minors. A facility that is safe, workers that are screened and trained, and space that is equipped for the age group using the space are items parents see often in a school or community environment. In a small church you may be convinced a volunteer application and background check is not needed since you know each other and function like a large extended family. A pre-trip checklist and a passenger manifest are basic documents many transportation fleet companies utilize for the safety of the people and vehicle being operated during a trip, and should be considered for a church's transportation usage.

Church-owned transportation can be a love/hate endeavor. Maybe you have experienced the van or bus breaking down during a trip and know the frustrations of owning a vehicle that is old or is not used on a regular basis. Your church should consider your plan for maintaining vehicles you own. You also should have guidelines for drivers of vehicles used by the church. You should consider the insurance and legality of vehicles owned, rented, or used by church members for church events, and whether or not your church carries liability insurance for these three types of vehicle usage. A checklist before each trip and a passenger manifest are basic documents that many fleet companies utilize for safety of the people and vehicle being operated.

Insurance to cover the ministry and facilities and any liabilities for the ministry your church conducts is an issue worthy of consideration. Do you carry coverage for staff, volunteers, buildings, furnishings, and overall liability of the ministry you conduct each week? Although insurance carriers and premiums vary by region and amount of insured coverage, a few basic considerations should be understood. A wise church layman once stated to me during a meeting that insurance companies exists for two reasons: to collect premiums and deny claims because it is a profitable business. The insurance binder for your policy may have exclusions, limits to coverage, and loopholes where they can deny claims. Due to these reasons, some special events may require your church to purchase a one-time special event policy to cover inflatables for the fall festival or whitewater rafting trip.

One area of consideration for your church is the distribution of keys to the facility. Many churches freely give out keys to church members, which can lead to facilities being left unlocked or things removed or taken that are needed at church. Church members can feel entitled to supplies or property, and possession of a key sometimes gives an impression that permission is granted for their discretion. I have seen this occur, resulting in missing items that were needed during a weekend for the ministry we had planned. This also causes stewardship concerns with resources being taken without a ministry purpose.

Teach your people that while we are a collective part of the church, the items are not our individual property. A policy outlining what constitutes church use and how to request resources or the facility for personal use can help solve this issue. You need to have key leadership involved in this transition and to help draft the policy. You may have family reunions in your fellowship hall, birthday parties, baby or bridal showers, a family member's wedding, or another request more personal in nature. The list of all the reasons people have requested resources or a facility for their personal activity is long, including family, sports, arts, and even personal business ventures. Some of the requests have ministry potential but require the church to approve their event for the church calendar and many times provide proof of their own liability insurance. These personal or family types of events will occur whether the church facility is available or not, it is just convenient, clean, and usually cheap or free for people to use. You will need to determine with church leadership the scope of facility usage at the church. If you choose to let people reserve the space for free, an agreement for liability will need to be utilized. In addition, check with the insurance provider to determine what would merit a decline in coverage for non-church-related facility usage. If you are renting, then always require a formal agreement that outlines usage guidelines, clean-up fees, damage waiver, and proof of liability insurance at the amount needed for your facility.

Many resources exist for church administration from books, articles, and websites that can provide you with more detailed specifics in any of the areas mentioned in this chapter. I encourage you as you seek to deal with any of these key components to church administration to look at some additional resources that will aide you in the area of administration. The guiding documents of the church are a crucial aspect that will guide many other areas of church administration. These documents, in a digital and current form, are needed for your church; however, be sure you consult with your leaders and discover the current valid edition of these documents. In addition, I would seek the guidelines in place and voted on by the church to make changes and revise these documents. The qualifications for ministers, staff, leaders, and volunteers need to be clearly defined in your guiding documents. You need to be sure to follow the qualification guidelines for everyone in the organization. The safety and security of a church, her ministries, and those involved is not an easy process. When you factor the facilities, property, events, and people, you realize security and safety is a more involved process today than it has ever been for the church. Finances can make everyone a little tense at times, but specific guidelines and processes should be in place so your church's finances can be administered effectively.

The care you take to administer in the areas we have mentioned are important, but I believe the most important is following Jesus' mandate to protect the children around us from stumbling. Each week a problem can arise due to risk factors in a minor area of ministry due to the volunteers, the facility, or an outside threat. Safeguarding the ministry of your church with minors, no matter the size of the congregation and family culture that exists, should be a high priority. Transportation, insurance, and even the key policy for your facility can be areas of great stress but should be evaluated in light of your guiding documents and administered accordingly for best practices. Many ministers shy away from administration and utilize the "I don't deal with these issues" approach and believe the leaders, committees, or issues will solve themselves. I encourage you to deal with the issues one at a time and create best practices for your church. You cannot solve everything mentioned by one committee or in one business meeting. The work is not easy, but do not be overwhelmed as you strive to shepherd the flock. Being an overseer is not an easy task and many areas of administration are not glamorous, but the church needs ministers to help them accomplish the work effectively. I believe these key areas of administration can help you accomplish the work of your church more effectively.

Questions for discussion and reflection:

1. Consider conducting a review of your guiding documents and determining if they are current for your church. When was the last time the documents were updated for current issues you may deal with? Do you have any components that need revision or subtraction/addition?

2. What is the approved leadership structure for your church and ministries? Do you have more committees than are needed? Do you have committees that could transition to a leadership team for ministry?

3. When is the last time you did a walk around your property to determine concerns along the perimeter—as well as interior—that could be safety or security issues?

4. What financial safeguards does your church have in place? Does the church always follow their financial guidelines?

5. What process do you follow to recruit, vet, and train volunteers in your church?

6. If you have discovered several areas of concern, then create a list of priority and develop a plan that addresses these concerns strategically and over a period of time. You do not want to overwhelm your people with issues and concerns. What is a realistic timeline to address your concerns?

BIBLIOGRAPHY

Collins, Jim. *Good to Great*. New York: Harper Business, 2001.
Welch, Robert H. *Church Administration: Creating Efficiency for Effective Ministry*, 2nd ed. Nashville: B&H Academic, 2001.

8

Discipleship in Small Churches

HAL STEWART

I've always been a sports fan. In fact, outside of reading about church ministry or spiritual formation and spending time with my family, my hobby is watching sports, no matter what season of the year. I grew up playing basketball and fell in love with the idea of coaching it. My ultimate dream was to coach college basketball in the NCAA Final Four. This dream grew out of both my yearly devotion to watch the Atlantic Coast Conference Basketball Tournament, March Madness in college basketball, and my experience of playing on teams. I wanted to experience the entire process of leading a team to prepare to improve, to practice and plan to win, to learn from defeats, and share joy by achieving a shared mission. To accomplish this mission, it would take leadership and personal development by every player. I knew it would take belief, dedication, hard work, patience, and teamwork.

UNDERSTANDING GOD'S MISSION

After a season of running away from God's will, I finally surrendered into ministry and accepted God's call to serve him vocationally and my dream changed. As I studied Scripture, attended seminary, and grew in my devotion to God, my passion changed. I realized God's dream to reach the world with the gospel is fulfilled by the local church. And since God has always chosen to work through people to accomplish his mission, I could actually join in on God's mission. I still loved basketball and eventually coached high school basketball for seven years, but my perspective changed.

The mission that Jesus modeled fulfilled the greater plan of God. God's plan involves world evangelism. God intended to save people for himself and to build a church which would never perish. No one is excluded from his gracious purpose. Ultimately, his love is universal and demonstrated in that he died for all sins and all people. Yet, this evangelistic mission had an underlying requirement of disciple-making. Disciple-making is the intentional passing on of the biblical faith to another person. J. I. Packer's definition of discipleship most aptly explains God's mission with evangelistic and disciple-making understanding: "Grounding and growing God's people in the gospel and its implications for doctrine, devotion, duty, and delight."[1] The implications of the mission to make disciples impacts all pastoral leaders.

Brad Waggoner explains the mission to make fishers of men by saying, "We have too many leaders who appear to be more concerned about attracting a crowd than fostering genuine spiritual transformation among believers."[2] The personal mission of pastors is not just the preaching preparation and communication from the platform. When leading a small congregation, relational investment in people is crucial in imparting the mission. Without building a congregation through disciple-making, "Our churches will be a mile wide and an inch deep. . . . "[3]

VALUING GOD'S MISSION

Do you believe the church needs to recapture her original mission of making disciples of Jesus? Have you ever dreamt of how this can happen in your church? Regardless of how you answered these questions, God's will for your life is to fulfill the Great Commission. This means God's will is for you to make disciples. Several decades ago Bill Hull said, "The Great Commission has been worshipped, but not obeyed. The church has tried to get world evangelism without disciple-making."[4] This call to make disciples is the mission of all churches of every size. And no mission is

1. Packer, *Grounded in the Gospel*, 29.
2. Waggoner, *The Shape of Faith to Come*, 49.
3. Ibid., 49.
4. Hull, *The Disciple Making Pastor*, 23.

ever achieved without a leader who cast a vision to determine how far to take the mission. Have you dreamt of how far your church, regardless of size, can take God's mission?

Maybe you are dreaming of a lay leader and church discipleship culture saturated with mature followers of Christ, willing to do whatever it takes to further God's kingdom. Maybe you are dreaming of helping and watching lay leaders take steps of obedience, and accept leadership roles in your church. Maybe you are dreaming that parents in your church will make Christ-honoring decisions and model Jesus to their children. Whatever your dream is related to the process of disciple-making, remember that the process is filled with peaks and valleys, steps forward and steps backward, life in oasis and desert. Eugene Peterson's definition of discipleship is a timely reminder, "Discipleship is a long obedience in the same direction."[5]

SMALL-CHURCH LEADERSHIP

Small-church leadership is paramount. Small churches are really normal churches. The lifeblood of the Southern Baptist Convention (SBC) is dependent on the spiritual health of smaller churches. And corporate spiritual health of a church of any size is dependent upon discipling others into an abiding relationship with God. Therefore, they are extremely important in the mission to reach the world for Christ. The 2014 SBC Annual Church Profile (ACP) report revealed 89.33 percent of SBC churches have 250 or less in worship service[6] and 83 percent average less than 124 in Sunday school/small groups.[7] If small churches can return to the original mission, great impact for God can happen, and it can happen nationwide. Since most small churches are led by single staff or bivocational pastors, the weight of the mission and success of a church is largely dependent on their leadership.

Therefore, understanding of God's mission is relevant not only for churches of all sizes, but especially for individual pastors in small churches. So, small-church pastors need not accept the myth of "bigger is better" when comparing small churches to larger churches. Every church matters to God.

---

5. Peterson, *A Long Obedience in the Same Direction*, 17.

6. Bill Day, "Bivocational and Smaller Membership Church Council Report," n.p.

7. Ibid.

Author Karl Vaters referred to this myth as the "grasshopper myth."[8] Vaters explained:

> The grasshopper myth is the lie many small church leaders tell ourselves. We see big, bigger and megachurches popping up all over the place, then when we glance back at ourselves we seem like grasshoppers 'in our own eyes.' That's where the myth starts. Inside us. And that's where it has to end.[9]

This idea is derived from the Old Testament when the Hebrews were oh-so-close to the promised land. "All the people we saw were of great size . . . We seemed like grasshoppers in our own eyes, and we looked the same to them" (Num 13:32–33, NIV). Small-church leadership necessitates personal mission which is coalesced with God's mission. Otherwise, disciple-making leadership will be weak and ineffective, revealing a lack vision.

THE GREAT COMMISSION IS GOD'S MISSION

The mission of the church is revealed in some of Jesus' last words to his followers. The Great Commission mandate is "Go therefore and make disciples of all nations, baptizing them in the name of the Father and of the Son and of the Holy Spirit, teaching them to observe all that I have commanded you. And behold, I am with you always, to the end of the age" (Matt 28:19–20, ESV). Church leaders who recognize the significance of this biblical mandate envision the transformation of lives. Additionally, a transformation of culture in their church will permeate all ministries. Author and Philosopher Dallas Willard emphasized the mission to make disciples: "We have no other God-appointed business but this, and we must allow all else to fall away if it will.[10]

SMALL CHURCHES AND DISCIPLESHIP

Discipleship in small churches is no less important than discipleship in medium to larger churches. And certainly in a bivocational or single full-time staff context, an argument can be made that the necessity to disciple laymen is even more paramount. Resources are less, and personal responsibility is

8. Vaters, "The Grasshopper Myth," line 22.

9. Ibid., line 22.

10. Willard, *The Great Omission*, 225.

magnified. Yet God's greatest resource on earth is the church. So all leaders or churches big and small have people, as well as God's promise of the presence of the Holy Spirit. Few pastors would deny that discipleship is essential to the mission of the church. Some would argue that discipleship is *the* mission. Some have suggested that discipleship and evangelism are "two sides or the same coin."[11] Noting that 80 percent of Southern Baptist churches have less than 125 in weekly Sunday school attendance, Ray Gilder, national coordinator of the Bivocational Small Church Leadership Network (BSCLN), called on pastors and churches to "find your life by giving yourself away."[12]

The purposes of this chapter are to offer a biblical overview of discipleship, introduce a biblical model for discipleship, and offer some practical best practices for small-church pastors.

THE GREAT COMMISSION EXPLAINED

Here are four points of importance in considering this disciple-making mandate. These four components include three participles, which are going, baptizing, and teaching.[13] These are the means, method, and activity of making disciples. And one unifying action, which is to observe all that Jesus commanded. Church leaders are to include each of these components in any disciple-making strategy.

Evangelizing

First, "Go" is the *evangelism* verb for every disciple. The word actually means "as you are going," with a strong sense to fulfill the mission. In John 15:16, Jesus said, "You did not choose me, but I chose you, and appointed you that you should go and bring forth fruit, and that your fruit should remain" (NIV). Note that "fruit" follows "going." The Apostle John is not speaking of "the fruit of the Spirit," or the character descriptive fruit(s) mentioned elsewhere in Scripture. A person can bear all of those fruits without ever going anywhere. But if you are going to "fish for men," you must go to where the

---

11. Hull, *Conversion and Discipleship*, 88.
12. "Tusculum Hills to House Bivocational/Small Church Center," lines 25-26.
13. Ferguson, *Baptism in the Early Church*, 137.

fish live. Here's the point in this "Go" participle: God chooses and appoints his disciples to bear fruit and follow up by cultivation so the fruit remains.

Assimilating

Second, "Baptize" is the *assimilation* verb for every disciple. The word "baptize" pictures a disciple's incorporation into Christ, conferring being "in Christ" forevermore. Baptizing basically means to be identified with the death, burial, and resurrection of Christ (Rom 6:1–4). In Galatians 2:20 Paul says, "I am crucified with Christ." He is stating "I have been *and remain*." Similarly, for church membership in a community of believers, baptism is a one-time event in the life of the believer and identifies the disciple with Christ and his bride, the church.

Instructing

Third, "Teach" is the *instruction* verb for all disciples. The word "teach" means "as you are teaching" as a vital ongoing action for fulfilling the Great Commission. This type of teaching in the church should lead to the spiritual edification of the learners. Teaching includes both a didactic and imitation aspect to be most impactful. Similar to "going," this component reveals the importance of teaching every moment of every hour of every day of every week of every month of every year to fulfill the Great Commission.

Training

Lastly, training involves an application aspect. This educational training in the life of the church means to apply the commands in Scripture to the actions of believers. This is where the rubber meets the road, so to speak. The unifying action is the aim to help all disciples "observe all things I have commanded." The word "observe" means to obey or keep Christ's commandments. Helping disciples follow God in obedience is the necessary action. John Stott has noted, "Our failure to obey the implications of this command is the greatest weakness of evangelical Christians in the field of evangelism today."[14] This all-important training is the edification aspect of helping believers follow and obey Christ's commands.[15]

The Great Commission to make disciples has *evangelism, assimilation,* and *instruction* components. The overall unifying action is to *train* disciples to observe or obey. This truly is the biblical description of spiritual growth and offers a clear and compelling mission for every church. To make a disciple, first one has to win a person (a non-disciple) to Christ. Then the new disciple needs to grow or mature as a disciple, hence the instruction component. So "making disciples" stresses both evangelism and disciple-making, while necessitating a discipling process initiated by church action (table 1).

Table 1: Disciple-Making Training Continuum

People	Non-Disciple	New Disciple	Growing Disciple
Spiritual Condition	Unbelief	Belief	Growing into Maturity
Component	Evangelize	Assimilate	Instruct
Church Action	Win	Grow	Send

Holy Spirit Presence

Matthew 28:20 (NIV) states, "And surely I am with you always, to the very end of the age." There is an incredible promise of partnership for the church. Jesus' words "I am with you always" provide the church with incredible promise that the mission is supported by God's very presence. Jesus even emphasized the action of remaining in him by saying "without me you can do nothing" (John 15:5, NIV). Simply put, God is going to do his part in the salvific process. And God's work is promised in this "co-mission." This should embolden us to proclaim and disciple without fear or anxiety. This necessary work by the Holy Spirit is not only instrumental, but is required

14. Andrews, *The Complete Guide to Bible Translation*, 271.

15. Peter Wittstock includes 125 commands that are in the gospels. Wittstock, *Hear Him!*, 221–22. John Piper developed a list of over 500 commands and unified them into 50 chapters. Piper, *What Jesus Demands from the World*, 7–11.

for effective discipling in the church. No man can build God's church. And nothing can stop the building of God's church. So this promise of the presence of the Holy Spirit is foundational in explaining the Great Commission.

THE INTEGRATION OF LEADERSHIP IN THE CHURCH DISCIPLESHIP PROCESS

The local church consists of disciples of Jesus Christ, people who are on a spiritual journey to be like Jesus in every way (e.g., Eph 4:15, Rom 8:29). Does a disciple's spiritual journey lead to a form of leadership in the church? I suggest that it does, and most small-church pastors are looking for leaders. If this is so, where are the leaders in the small churches?

Perhaps Christian leadership as a gift and calling is a primary need in all churches. Aubrey Malphurs begins his book *Strategic Disciple Making* by asking the question, "What are we supposed to be doing?" [16] In the leadership development process, discipleship always proceeds leadership. Leadership is a by-product of discipleship.

Leaders are needed in all churches. And maybe even more so in a small-church setting. Should leaders not be disciples and disciple-makers? Jesus was a disciple-maker and a leader who reproduced his beliefs, character, and skills into the lives of his disciples. Many leadership principles were modeled in his life. Here are three examples.

16. Malphurs, *Strategic Disciple Making*, 5.

Table 2: Integration of Discipleship to Leadership

Discipleship Principle of Jesus	Explanation of the Principle	Leadership Principle of Jesus
All Believers Need Personal Development	Jesus saw unlimited potential in people, and often chose the people who were not particularly skilled. Jesus overlooked the selection of highly skilled individuals, something not taught today, and chose twelve ordinary men.	Choosing ordinary people to lead
Small Groups and Mentoring are More Effective than Preaching to Masses	Contemporary leadership principles teach to seize the momentum for growth. Breaking the law of momentum, Jesus forgoes preaching to the masses for secretly traveling to another city to proclaim his message (Mark 1:35–37). Consistently, he settled the hype surrounding his ministry by saying, "See that you say nothing to anyone" (Mark 1:44).	Investing in lives of people
Submission to God and Others	The disciples are concerned about position and prominence, but Jesus tells them discipleship involves a willingness to suffer, and it also means a life of service for others (Mark 10:38–44).	Serve, rather than be served, as a leader.

Jesus' Leadership Principle is Discipleship

Jesus' leadership is a model for the church today. His leadership example breaks many traditional leadership laws, and aligns with many as well. Bill Hybels studied the techniques Jesus used knowing that Jesus practiced leadership development. All of His techniques were ultimately focusing on reproducing faithful followers, or disciples. Leadership principles can be gleamed from the life of Jesus.

After observing Jesus' leadership style, Hybels admitted, "I believe that, most of the time, the laws of leadership and the teachings of Scripture—particularly regarding embracing people living far from God and discipling those who have already made a faith decision—dovetail nicely."[17] He then added, "Jesus consistently manifested what we might consider traditional leadership laws throughout his ministry; he cast and consistently

17. Hybels, *When Leadership and Discipleship Collide*, 46.

reinforced a God-given, crystal-clear vision. He was perpetually 'on purpose'; he poured into his team until the mission poured out of them."[18] Discipleship is a viable model for leadership, particularly in the local church setting. Hybels concluded, "In those rare cases when the human laws of leadership and the scriptural demands of discipleship do collide, decide on the side of discipleship every time. *Decide on the side of discipleship every single time*."[19] Overall, Jesus' discipleship ministry can be broken down into four progressions, as listed in the table.

Table 3: Jesus' Progression of Discipling Leadership[20]

Progressions of Discipling Leaders	Explanation
Directing	Jesus provides specific direction and closely monitors task accomplishment.
Coaching	Jesus continues to direct and closely monitor task accomplishment, but also explains decisions, solicits suggestions, and supports progress.
Supporting	Jesus facilitates and supports disciples' efforts toward task accomplishment and shares responsibility for decision-making with them.
Delegating	Jesus turns over responsibility for decision-making and problem-solving to disciples.

This model of leading and discipling was incorporated into every aspect of his ministry. His style of leadership can be clearly seen in the call to those first fisherman when he said, "Follow me, and I will make you fishers of men" (Mark 4:19).

Paul's Model of Discipleship and Leadership

In 2 Timothy, for example, Paul alludes to the importance and purpose of discipleship four times (1:5; 2:1; 3:10, 14). "You then, my child," states the Apostle Paul, "be strengthened by the grace that is in Christ Jesus, and what you have heard from me in the presence of many witnesses entrust

18. Ibid., 47–48.

19. Ibid., 50.

20. Blanchard, et al, *Leadership And The One-Minute Manager*, 30. This model was adapted from Blanchard's four different leadership styles.

to faithful men who will be able to teach others also" (2 Tim 2:1–2). Four generations of discipleship emerge from this one verse. Paul taught Timothy who was instructed to teach faithful men to duplicate the process in the lives of other men.

Through the local church body disciples are produced. Since the New Testament church was intentional about making disciples, modern churches should follow that thread. A. Boyd Luter Jr. cites, "In-depth discipleship training was used to equip the foundational leaders of the New Testament church (Eph 2:20). Thus it is logical that churches today think of discipleship as a step toward developing qualified leadership."[21]

DISCIPLE-MAKING APPROACHES

The responsibility for making disciples rests on God, the church, and individual commitment. Malphurs concludes, "Whereas each individual is responsible for making a choice as to whether he or she will be a growing disciple, the church as a body is responsible for helping its people grow as disciples."[22] Discipleship is public and corporate, as well as personal and individual. Hull believes that the best way to create disciples is for individual and church disciple-making to become one.[23]

The application of the strategy includes four approaches to disciple-making. Any single approach has both strengths and weaknesses. Some of the approaches are dependent upon the age and season of life of people involved. A comprehensive disciple-making approach in the local church is best accomplished by using a variety of approaches. These four approaches are not exclusive. A church of any size may use discipling methods from one, two, three, or all four of these approaches. In fact, I fully believe a variety of disciple-making approaches is most beneficial in the application of a strategy.

21. Luter Jr., "Discipleship and the Church," 272.
22. Malphurs, *Strategic Disciple Making*, 42.
23. Hull, *Disciple Making Pastor*, 34.

Table 4: Disciple-Making Approaches

Approach	Platform-Dictated	Program Driven	Personal Ministry	People Multiplied
Church Discipling Venues	• Corporate Worship • Large groups	• Group Life • Short-term Courses • Leadership Training	• Membership Classes • Individual and Guided Service	• Mentoring • Micro-groups • Family Led
Christ's Model	Jesus preaching to the crowds in the gospels.	Jesus teaching the small crowds and training followers.	Jesus investing in the twelve disciples and sending out workers for service.	Jesus mentoring Peter, James, and John as the inner circle.
Discipleship Lifestyle	Compartmentalized Engagement	Affinity within Groups	Assimilated Service and Mission	Integrated and Holistic Lifestyle
Commitment	Nominal Attendee	Participating Member	Personal Investment Disciple	High-Impact Disciple

Discipling others does not just happen—it calls for intentionality, planning (strategy), prayer, and constantly discerning the voice of the Holy Spirit in the discipling relationship. Disciple-making can happen in groups, families, churches, or one-on-one relationships. Discipling others can be done in various ways and the intended results normally take a lot of time. Keep in mind that the evangelism component must always be a primary consideration. Certainly, the first step in the disciple-making process is conversion (salvation).

Platform-Dictated

This disciple-making approach reaches or directs the widest section of members and attendees in the church setting. On the macro-group level, this approach occurs during the primary worship service and is often modeled in secondary services, such as Sunday evenings and Wednesday evenings. On the micro level, this approach even happens in traditional Sunday school classes that meet and are led through a didactic style of teaching, rather than a dialogue style. In the mind of the preacher, disciple-making takes place every week in the primary worship service of the church when the preaching occurs. Certainly there is a uniqueness and openness for the Holy Spirit to move in hearts during the proclamation of God's word. And most believers are deeply influenced by the worship experience and by sermons in particular. The preacher can set the disciple-making tone for the church by modeling how to read and interpret the Bible for life transformation.

SUGGESTED PRACTICES

PROVIDE LISTENING GUIDES. Plan ahead and provide a preaching/teaching outline for taking notes to all attenders. Also, providing more study notes and meaningful application can aid the learner's understanding and help those who are more mature believers. On the micro-group level this does happen when learners are provided a study guide for weekly lessons; yet, this rarely occurs during worship services, although some preachers do post their notes online for church members and attenders.

INFORMAL AND FORMAL SURVEYING. Another potential practice is to periodically survey worshippers to see what disciple-making needs are most pressing. Expository preachers would be opposed to this idea, but at the very least their application of the text can be formatted to address the individual concerns and needs. Also, preaching a sermon series on a given topic or book of the Bible over several weeks provides repetition over a short period of time, which will keep a topic in the forefront and allow disciples to experience real life-change in that one area rather than bombarding them with a new topic each week.

DIALOGUE WITH CHURCH MEMBERS. Providing a forum for discussion of the sermon topic and how it might apply to one's life would allow deeper reflection and possible long-term retention. Some churches provide an email address, blog forum, or phone number to text. This creates a means to discuss the sermon/discipleship topic in an informal manner. Additionally, this might be something a family or small group does together as directed by a printed guide. And this guide could be used in other disciple-making approaches (program-driven or people multiplied).

WEAKNESSES

Some weaknesses are inherent. There is no measurement of commitment, other than an invitation at the end of the service, for those who attend. Additionally, it is hard to follow up with attenders and subsequently to measure life-change. Therefore, accountability is difficult if not impossible. An attender's transparency with respect to their personal issues is minimally observed. For the preacher, he is typically able to address only one type of spiritual issue at a time during the sermon, which means it's difficult to simultaneously target the discipling needs of every person. Basically, there are attenders of all different levels of spiritual maturity who are listening to the sermon, which does lend itself to full dependence on the Holy Spirit to convict of sin and righteousness.

Program-Driven

This disciple-making approach can also reach a wide section of church members and attendees because of multiple classes and meeting times. This approach is systematic programming with a chosen curriculum that includes a scope and sequence. Examples of program-driven are Sunday school and small groups, which tend to be attended by many church members. Therefore this discipling approach can be very practical and efficient for the purpose of fulfilling the church mission to make disciples. It can also include smaller groups that meet for a specific period of weeks, with either the goal to multiply or restart later. These groups provide organization and stability to the discipleship endeavor. Use of published curriculum allows for a uniform discipleship experience for attendees and is especially useful for teaching through books of the Bible and specific topics. The specific topics can be needs-based for adults, which improves the desire and motivation to participate. Basically this approach is any ongoing open or closed group that is programmed to fulfill the mission of making disciples.

SUGGESTED PRACTICES

PROGRAM YOUR MINISTRIES. Accept the fact that a programming approach does work because it's basically an organized means to fulfill the Great Commission. So, clear disciple-making expectations for the program-driven effort require planning, organizing, leading, and evaluating. Examining the discipling needs of people of all ages reveals that the most structured programming begins with preschoolers and becomes less structured as high school students enter adulthood.

Define a disciple. Your church needs a succinct definition of a disciple and how a disciple lives. The definition informs the programming. This will guide how your programs will move people closer to that target. Learn the context of the church to find out what the life needs are and what discipleship topics are most pressing. This practice means you should train your program leaders to be spiritual disciplers through the programs they lead. The programs exist to create and develop disciples, so knowing the definition and characteristics of a disciple are necessary.

Needs-based programming. Rather than offer strictly age-based courses for adults through a traditional Sunday school or groups approach, give participants a selection of topics offered simultaneously. So, the Sunday school or groups end up complementing the needs-based offerings. There are four basic areas of needs-based programming to train and disciple adults. These areas include dating and marriage, parenting, money and finances, and vocational discovery. These types of discipling opportunities meet people where there basic needs and questions exist. Offering these once a year on a rotational schedule will prove productive in a programmed approach.

Weaknesses

The primary weakness is programming undoes itself. What do I mean by that? Simply put, hard work, accountability, volunteer recruitment, and renewing of mission/vision is a continuous effort! And over time, a good program will always require review and adjustment in order to revitalize itself. Additionally, overemphasis on numbers and tasks, rather than people, is a constant temptation for leadership. While programming does provide the metrics of growth for evaluation and review, our effort and ministry can become less about ministering to people. Lastly, typically the Sunday school approach, which is a programmed approach, requires building and space. Some smaller churches simply do not have the space ratios to match worship seats and parking to sustain long-term growth. There are some solutions such as moving to two Sunday schools to help, but unless designated space for preschool and children is increased, this will not resolve limited growth.

Personal Ministry

This disciple-making approach can reach many members and attendees of your church with increased time, effort, and intentionality. It may take the form of coaching or periodic training events, such as membership classes or leadership training. This approach takes shape by helping people understand the role and function of the church, and accepting the call to serve in the life of the church. All disciples are saved to serve! So, each person has been crafted or designed by God for a unique purpose (Eph 2:10). A holistic approach for personal development is needed for church members to understand God's plan and purpose for their lives. Often this approach includes the following: a spiritual gifts inventory, a questionnaire to determine a person's personality, finding out a person's passion and interests, and examining life experiences. All of these aspects contribute to a person's unique design.[24]

SUGGESTED PRACTICES

MEMBERSHIP CLASS. Offer a membership class that teaches all new church members the importance of membership. A membership workshop needs to include teaching the core doctrinal beliefs, meaning, and application of the gospel, identifying the approaches to discipleship in the body, and including a personal calling for ministry and missions for every church member. A church member's unique design for ministry and missions can be identified and appropriated for church service when the membership workshop is completed.

AIM FOR THE HEART. One reason this approach is successful is it aims to answer the heart's question of "What am I here for?" Fulfilling the purpose and mission through the local church should be the aim of every church member. Therefore this approach takes longer to implement, requires some small group and individual feedback, and is a sequential growth process.

---

24. Examples of this type of personal design include Rick Warren's S.H.A.P.E. and Gene Wilkes' S.E.R.V.E. Warren, *Purpose Driven Church*; Wilkes, *Jesus on Leadership*.

As the heart of the disciple accepts, values, and receives the answer to the question "What am I here for?" deployment into ministry occurs. When the heart of a disciple accepts, values, and receives the understanding, the result is deployment into ministry.

Implement a Leadership Pipeline. The strong emphasis on assimilation into ministry and volunteer positions, individual gift development and deployment in ministry, and eventual multiplication results in more leaders. Effective levels of accountability and feedback from church leaders lead disciples to volunteer for leadership slots in the church. In turn, this disciple-making approach will produce leaders who can serve on ministry teams and contribute to the teaching ministry of the church.

Weaknesses

Like the previous disciple-making approaches, church leadership can fall into the deception of focusing on the process, rather than the individual. The process of finding a unique personal design is important and instrumental, but the primary focus should remain on God's mission. The individual surveys and instruments are not foolproof. The heart is deceptive (Jer 17:9) and sometimes a person's desire to serve in a specific ministry area may just impair the discovery process. Additionally, this approach requires constant evaluation in order to be highly effective. Church leaders must have places of ministry for people to serve in and through. In a small-church setting, this may require the pastor to allow and empower additional ministries to begin with lay leaders. Furthermore, this disciple-making approach is a foundational aspect of the church's life because it is the entry point into leadership development.

People Multiply

This is the highest level of intentional disciple-making, aimed for the multiplication of disciples. This approach is best applied for the greatest results when the pastor models this to the church. In other words, the pastor leads by example. Basically, the disciple leader (pastor) recruits one to five people to disciple for the course of a year or more. This is a closed, gender-based group (unless it is family-based), which allows for authentic conversations and transparency regarding growth and shortcomings. The men or women who participle know up-front they eventually will lead their own group. Then parents take ownership of the spiritual development of their children to the extent of having systematic and intentional times of discipleship. Many of the same benefits as the personal design approach exist, but deeper and more powerful results can be expected. Yet, this does not replace the other three approaches, but enhances and completes them. Due to the closed nature of the group, it is not necessarily as evangelistic like the other approaches.

SUGGESTED PRACTICES

MENTORING. This is a dynamic relationship whereby a maturing believer is willing to invest on a regular basis in the life of one younger, growing believer. This approach helps to integrate life and mission for the individual believer. The rise of technology and decay of the family structure have increased the necessity to bond through learning. Mentoring offers a personal and intentional growth plan for disciples. This disciple-making approach builds on the foundation of Christ in lives (1 Cor 3:10–15) by warning and teaching in wisdom (Col 1:28–29) and by example (Phil 3:17). Since there is only one person being mentored, growth may occur more rapidly due to the focused, intentional investment of the mentor.

MICROGROUPS. These are disciple-making groups of two to five people that are characterized by a sincere commitment to engage with others in the group for an extended period of time for both personal spiritual growth and investment in others' lives. Typically, this group is made up of members who are in similar stages of life, and have a strong affinity toward each other. And this type of group is less hierarchical in structure than mentoring. High-level commitment includes accountability, transparency, and confidentiality. The ultimate aim of such a group is reproduction. A group may meet weekly for twelve to eighteen months and then multiply into more groups with the original group members leading the new groups.

FAMILY DISCIPLING GROUPS. These groups are created within family units. There are two types of family discipling groups: husband and wife, and parents with children at home. First, spouses decide that spiritual growth is so important that they devote themselves to growing closer to God and together through one-on-one discipleship. Normally, the husband takes the spiritual leadership ownership of this mentoring relationship. Second, parents take ownership of the spiritual development of their children at home to the extent of having systematic and intentional times of disciple-making. This varies depending on the ages and number of children in the home. Often this type of discipleship can include follow-up and review of the content from other discipleship approaches. An example of this would be family devotions based on the program-driven weekly lessons in group life.

WEAKNESSES

The weaknesses of this discipleship approach are primarily two-fold. First, this approach takes lots of time and deeper levels of commitment. On the hierarchal mentoring, there is necessary leadership development and continual follow-up with encouragement and motivation. On the microgroup and family discipling, people may grow spiritually at different rates. Thus, slowing the group down or requiring the group or family to focus on a single concern or issue. Second, this approach is difficult to measure. The fruit for this approach could take months or years to bear out. So, this approach is slow and done alone by excluding the other approaches, and would result in an inward focus that neglects a spiritually lost world.

DEVELOPING A CULTURE FOR DISCIPLESHIP

Implementing all four discipleship approaches and the suggested practices will begin a culture change at your church. But those alone will not be enough. The approaches create structure and intentionality that aligns with the mission of the church. Yet, there is more for the pastor to consider and develop in the church setting. You can expect steady and solid growth either spiritually and/or numerically:

1. *Everything in your job description is a form of discipleship.* The saying is true, "more is caught than taught." This is especially true in discipling others. The tendency is to lead only by teaching and preaching in the platform-directed approach. While this is a necessity, the pastor needs to choose discipling moments. For instance, guiding the deacons and leading committees or ministry teams are opportunities to disciple. Often these can take the form of personal ministry approaches to discipleship. The pastoral leader should integrate God's truths via

Scripture into all meetings and ministry moments. Just embed the Bible in everything you and the church does. And he should lead by example in every servant leadership moment.

2. *Personal growth and spiritual reproduction are related.* Simply put, every pastor needs to be vitally concerned and focused on his personal spiritual growth. This means consistent time in prayer, Bible reading, Scripture memory, solace and silence, and journaling. These spiritual disciplines can increase awareness of divine opportunities to disciple others and share your faith. And the repeated acting of one's will in these areas will develop habits, and form godly, Spirit-induced character.

3. *Be willing to empower others to lead.* It's your job to get people moving into these different disciple-making approaches, but you can't lead them all. Empower others to lead. The timing for enlisting others is crucial because there is typically a season of casting the vision to make disciples and it is only completed when others take up the mantle of ownership of the vision.

When I consider the disciple-making task ahead of the church, I'm always reminded of God's promises. I'm amazed at his faithfulness, and when I consider the depth of God's commitment to me, I feel woefully inadequate. And in that inadequacy, I know that by his grace and power I can fulfill his call on my life to disciple others. If you're like me, often I feel the discipling of people is not moving along as fast as I want it to, or the four approaches are not all working at a high spiritual level, and I've needed to balance God's timing and my effort to accomplish the mission. In my experience, it takes several years of working and serving a local church to begin to see and feel a change in a discipling culture by implementing the stated approaches. In the book *Outliers,* Malcolm Gladwell established a standard with lots of research that most things/people don't become great unless 10,000 hours are put into it.[25] At fifty hours per week (most small-church or bivocational pastors work more), it would take about five years to create a discipleship culture, if it solely depended on you.

---

25. Gladwell, *Outliers*, 40.

GOD'S GLORY—THE UNIFYING PRINCIPLE

Is your mission to fulfill the Great Commission? Or is your mission to glorify God? Or both? Leading discipleship ministries in local churches take time, energy, leadership, and a variety of disciple-making approaches. You need to accept that when we give our very best for God's glory, he is satisfied. I realized the unifying principle of disciple-making was the biblical idea to make God's name known in the world. In other words, the unifying principle is the glory of God. The advancement of God's kingdom, his reign and rule on earth, happens through his bride, the church. The Apostle John shared this in John 15:8 "My father is glorified by this: that you produce much fruit and so prove to be my disciples" (NASB). God the Father is glorified when disciples make disciples. This carries along with it the incredible aspect of discipling those who accept Christ to the point of becoming reproducing disciples. When this happens, God's fame increases across the world. His kingdom advances into a lost and dying world. Is your dream to advance God's mission? The idea to give God the glory includes the volitional choice to produce fruit by discipling others.

BIBLIOGRAPHY

Andrews, Edward D. *The Complete Guide to Bible Translation*. Cambridge, OH: Christian Publishing House, 2012.

Blanchard, Ken, et al. *Leadership and the One-Minute Manager*. New York: William Morrow and Company, 1985.

Day, Bill. "Bivocational and Smaller Membership Church Council Report." http://www.sbc.net/advisoryCouncilReports/pdf/Bivo-SmallChurch2016.pdf.

Ferguson, Everett. *Baptism in the Early Church: History, Theology, and Liturgy in the First Five Centuries*. Grand Rapids: Wm. B. Eerdmans, 2009.

Gladwell, Malcolm. *Outliers: The Story of Success*. New York: Little, Brown and Company, 2008.

Hull, Bill. *Conversion and Discipleship*. Grand Rapids: Zondervan, 2016.

———. *The Disciple Making Pastor*. Old Tappan, NJ: Fleming Revell, 1988.

Hybels, Bill. *When Leadership and Discipleship Collide*. Grand Rapids: Zondervan, 2006.

Luter Jr., Boyd. "Discipleship and the Church," *Bibliotheca Sacra* 137 (1980), 137-272.

Malphurs, Aubrey. *Strategic Disciple Making*. Grand Rapids: Baker, 2009.

Packer, J.I. *Grounded in the Gospel*. Grand Rapids: Baker, 2010.

Peterson, Eugene. *A Long Obedience in the Same Direction*. Downers Grove, IL: IVP Academic, 2010.

Piper, John. *What Jesus Demands from the World*. Wheaton, IL: Crossway, 2006.

"Tusculum Hills to House Bivocational/Small Church Center." *SBC Life* (September 2014). http://www.sbclife.net/Articles/2014/09/sla13.

Vaters, Karl. "The Grasshopper Myth," *Pivot* (blog), *Christianity Today*, http://www.christianitytoday.com/karl-vaters/about/books.html?paging=off.

Waggoner, Brad J. *The Shape of Faith to Come*. Nashville: Broadman & Holman, 2008.

Willard, Dallas. *The Great Omission: Reclaiming Jesus's Essential Teachings on Discipleship*. New York: HarperCollins, 2006.

Wittstock, Peter. *Hear Him! The One Hundred and Twenty-Five Commands of Jesus*. Longwood, FL: Xulon, 2004.

SECTION 4

Pastoral Qualifications
for Small-Church Ministry

9

Personal Spiritual Health
of a Smaller Church Pastor

PATRICK WEAVER

Former Major League Baseball player and manager Gene Mauch was credited with saying, "You can't lead anyone further than you have gone yourself." This statement rings true considering Mauch never made it to a World Series. As a player, he never came close to winning a championship, but as a coach, he did have a couple of opportunities. In the 1982 American League Championship Series (ALCS), Mauch's California Angels team missed going to the World Series by one game, and in 1986 Mauch's team was only one strike away from winning the ALCS before the relief pitcher gave up a home run in the bottom of the ninth inning to the Boston Red Sox spurring a comeback in extra innings. The Red Sox would go on to win that series, and Mauch would never come that close to winning a World Series again. As a coach, Mauch was unable to lead his players beyond where he had been.

Pastors, especially pastors of smaller-membership churches, face this same problem every day. Pastors cannot lead their church further than they have gone themselves, particularly in the area of spiritual disciplines and their intentional time spent with the Lord. Simply considering the schedule of pastors serving in these settings is overwhelming. If they are bivocational, there are work obligations, family obligations, and church responsibilities. Others are fully-funded pastors but probably do not have the staff devoted to tasks as simple as printing the bulletin and taking out the trash. Also, pastoral responsibilities still need to take place: sermon preparation, Bible study preparation, meetings, hospital visits, weddings, funerals, and discipleship all add to the pastor's busy schedule. In the midst of a challenging schedule, pastors have been called first and foremost to walk in relationship with Christ.

The call to be a follower of Christ will always supersede the call to be a leader in the church. Many of the leaders God revealed in Scripture were men and women who sought to walk with God before they desired to be good leaders. Consider the qualifications for Noah to lead his family to build the Ark: "Noah was a righteous man, blameless in his generation. Noah *walked* with God" (Gen 6:9, ESV, emphasis added). Though little is known about him, Enoch had a similar relationship with God. Enoch walked so close to the Lord that he was able to avoid experiencing death because he "pleased" the Lord (Gen 5:24; Heb 11:5).

Moses was an unlikely choice to lead the people of Israel out of Egypt. He was born of slaves and adopted by Pharaoh's daughter. He fled from Egypt as a young man after murdering an Egyptian guard, but even through these flaws, the last words ever written about Moses were "there has not arisen a prophet since in Israel like Moses, whom the LORD knew face to face" (Deut 34:10, ESV).

King David also had a different set of qualifications to be the leader of Israel. When Samuel came to anoint one of Jesse's sons to be the next king, Jesse did not even bother asking his youngest son to meet with Samuel because surely God would not pick this scrawny shepherd boy to be the next king. He did not fit the part, and he did not look the part, but God told Samuel, "For the Lord sees not as man sees: man looks on the outward appearance, but the Lord looks on the heart" (1 Sam 16:7). Whether it was Noah, Enoch, Moses, David, or the host of other Old Testament leaders, God first cared about their hearts before their ministry.

The same examples are found in the New Testament as well. In Jesus' earthly ministry he both demonstrated and taught what it meant to prioritize a relationship with the Father over everything else. As a matter of fact, Jesus taught his followers how to be disciples, not leaders. The greatest leadership characteristic he taught them was how to follow. As disciples, their relationship goal was to seek after Christ above all else. Jesus' command was simple, "Follow me" (Matt 4:19, 8:22, 9:9, 16:24, 19:21; Mark 1:17, 2:14, 8:34, 10:21; Luke 5:27, 9:23, 9:59, 18:22; John 1:43, 12:26, 21:19).

Jesus made it clear that a relationship with him would be difficult. Occasionally, people would have to leave careers, family, and friends to be obedient to the relationship he had called them to enter. They would have to go against the cultural norms. They would have to forsake the ways of the world to follow a Nazarene through the desert for three years, learning everything they could about the Lord. Jesus was able to teach them how to follow because he was busy following as well. The Bible is clear, Jesus had all authority and all power. Jesus was truly God and truly man. He was the second person of the Trinity, yet he laid it all aside. He stepped off his throne in glory to be born in a stable. Why? So, he could come live the life we could not live and die the death we deserve. That was Jesus' mission and purpose, but he did so because of his devotion to the Father. On the night of his arrest, Jesus made it clear that he valued his relationship with the Father more than anything else. He prayed, "My Father, if it be possible, let this cup pass from me; nevertheless, not as I will, but as you will" (Matt 26:39). Just as Jesus' earthly ministry came from an overflow of his relationship with the Father, our work in ministry should originate from the overflow of our relationship with Christ.

The Apostle Paul also understood the priority of a relationship with Christ. When Paul wrote to the church in Philippi, he thanked them for their contribution to the ministry, and he explained why he preached the gospel, "For me to live is Christ, and die is gain" (Phil 1:21). The reason Paul ministered was that his life had been encompassed by Christ. He was willing to lose all of his earthly gain and earthly position to know Christ (Phil 3:7–8). His only goal was to please Christ in his work and spend eternity with Christ in heaven (Phil 3:13–14). Jesus completely changed Paul's life on that Damascus road. Paul left on a journey to persecute Christians and returned ready to tell the world of the grace, mercy, and salvation only in Jesus. Paul's words throughout the New Testament give an indication that his greatest joy in life was not the people he had won to the Lord, the churches he had planted, the knowledge he had obtained, or the family he was born into. His greatest joy was that Christ had a relationship with him. Throughout his ministry, Paul demonstrated the same attitude of Christ. A successful ministry is not determined by numerical growth, but a life that is crucified in Christ (Gal 2:20).

Aspiring pastors and new pastors have understood that to serve the Lord in ministry, they will take every step possible to equip themselves for the work of ministry. Many will go to seminary, others will surround themselves with experienced pastors, others will read books, and others will attend conferences, but the precursor for leading the people of God has always been to walk faithfully in relationship with God. Charles Spurgeon taught this same idea to his students at The Pastors' College. In 1881, Spurgeon wrote to these aspiring pastors:

> We are in a certain sense, our own tools, and therefore must keep ourselves in order . . . It will be in vain for me to stock my library, or organise societies, or project schemes, if I neglect the culture of myself; for books, and agencies, and systems, are only remotely the instruments of my holy calling; my own spirit, soul, and body, are my nearest machinery for sacred sacrifice; my spiritual faculties, and my inner life, are my battle axe and weapons of war.[1]

Spurgeon identified that the tools for a successful ministry are not found in books, knowledge, or relationships but by each pastor focusing on their spiritual walk with Christ.

When Paul wrote his first letter to Timothy he gave a detailed description for the overseer, or pastor, of the church (1 Tim 3:1–7). Pastors were to be men who were above reproach with no fault found in them. Pastors were to lead their families well because God was putting them in a position to lead God's family. Pastors were to be self-controlled, respectable, hospitable, gentle, and non-divisive. Except "being able to teach," the role of the pastor was more focused on a pastor's character and spirituality than on his physical abilities. So how does a pastor accomplish such an overwhelming task? Paul told Timothy, "Rather train yourself for godliness; for while bodily training is of some value, godliness is of value in every way" (1 Tim 4:7b–8, ESV).

PRACTICING THE SPIRITUAL DISCIPLINES

The idea of discipline does not sound fun or enjoyable on any level. Training to be the best at a skill or to change a habit is difficult. Many people have tried the dreaded New Year's resolution. The idea sounds simple, but the execution is always poor. In a 2002 John Norcross study, he determined that

---

1. Spurgeon, *Lectures to My Students*, 1–2.

approximately 25 percent of all New Year's resolutions have failed by the end of the first week.[2] The reason resolutions fail is because they lack direction. In his book, *Spiritual Disciplines for the Christian Life*, Donald Whitney said, "Discipline without direction is drudgery."[3] Just like a professional athlete has a specific training regimen for his skill, every Christian should have an intentional, specific training regimen that assists them in growing.

For followers of Christ, the training regimen is spiritual disciplines. Classic spiritual disciplines include activities such as Scripture reading, prayer, evangelism, Sabbath, fasting, ministry service, and worship. While the practice will differ, the principles remain the same for all.

Spiritual Disciplines are a Tool to Help Train in Godliness

One will never be more like Christ unless they train. Dallas Willard said, "A baseball player who expects to excel in the game without adequate exercise of his body is no more ridiculous than the Christian who hopes to be able to act in the manner of Christ when put to the test without the appropriate exercise in godly living."[4] The work completed towards godliness is necessary for living as a follower of Christ. Jesus took the long road to preparing for the ministry that God had called him to complete. Very little is told about Jesus as an adolescent except for the Passover trip in which Jesus accompanied Joseph and Mary to Bethlehem. Upon finishing the Passover celebration, Jesus went missing from the caravan traveling back home. "After three days they found him in the temple, sitting among the teachers, listening to them and asking them questions" (Luke 2:46, ESV). Just being allowed to sit with these rabbis and discuss the Torah demonstrates the level of training Jesus had undergone to understand the real meaning of the teachings found in the Torah. Jesus was taking the necessary steps to prepare for ministry.

Jesus would continue to grow up in obscurity, silently preparing for the time when God the Father released him into ministry. After his public ministry had begun, Jesus continued to demonstrate how to practice biblical spiritual disciplines. He prayed and fasted after being baptized by John. He frequently retreated to spend time with the Father. Jesus' ministry

2. Norcross, "Auld Lang Syne," 398.
3. Whitney, *Spiritual Disciplines for the Christian Life*, 1.
4. Willard, *The Spirit of the Disciplines: Understanding How God Changes Lives*, 4–5.

was dependent on a continuous interaction with the Father. Training to be more like God never ends because the battle never ends.

Spiritual Disciplines Prepare for Spiritual Warfare

The greatest battle a Christian will ever face is not against physical forces, but "against the spiritual forces of evil in the heavenly places" (Eph 6:12, ESV). Therefore, the tools needed to fight this battle are not physical either. This truth is even more evident in the life of a minister. Little distracts from the mission of God more than a minister who succumbs to the temptation of Satan. Peter reminded the ministers and elders in dispersion, "Be sober minded; be watchful. Your adversary, the devil, prowls around like a roaring lion, seeking someone to devour" (1 Pet 5:8, ESV). The proclamation of the gospel and the advancement of the church is a vicious battle. When Paul explained how to stand against the "schemes of the devil," he used the example of a soldier going into battle (Eph 6:10–19). The armor of God is the battle gear needed to stand against the devil, and that armor is developed through the practice of spiritual disciplines.

Jesus demonstrated how to use spiritual disciplines to stand against the schemes of Satan when Satan tempted him in the wilderness (Matt 4:1–11; Mark 1:12–13; Luke 4:1–13). Jesus had just been baptized by John and was preparing to begin his earthly ministry. Jesus, being in direct communication with the Spirit (prayer), was led into the wilderness to be tempted by Satan. To prepare for the temptation, he did not eat anything for forty days and nights (fasting). When Jesus reached the end of those forty days, Satan came and tried to convince Jesus to turn rocks into bread, to worship him, and to throw himself from the cliff so the angels could come and save him. In each of these situations, Jesus declined by responding with Scripture (Bible intake). Jesus was able to overcome Satan because he had a genuine relationship with the Father that was demonstrated through spiritual disciplines. Pastor, as a minister of the gospel you will never overcome the spiritual warfare that will take place in your life unless you are proactive in knowing Jesus. Spiritual disciplines prepare for spiritual warfare.

Spiritual Disciplines are not Tools for Legalism

The temptation with spiritual disciplines is to allow them to become Pharisaical in their practice. An intentional time to read Scripture and pray can quickly become another task to check off the daily list of "How to be a Good Christian" if we lose focus of the goal. Again, the end goal of practicing spiritual disciplines is godliness. Donald Whitney pointed out that spiritual disciplines are means and not ends. Whitney said, "So while we cannot be godly without the practice of the Disciplines, we can practice the Disciplines without being godly if we see them as ends and not means."[5] It does not matter if Christians pray for exactly an hour a day or read the Bible in a year. These tasks are good goals to have, but to know Jesus is a better goal. Never allow prayer, Bible intake, fasting, evangelism, missions, or any other spiritual discipline to become a tool used by Satan to make you feel guilty. As followers of Christ, we are saved by grace and not by works. Spiritual disciplines should never to be used as a means for legalism.

Spiritual Disciplines Lead to a Life of Holiness and Self-control

Pastors are men of God who have been called to shepherd the church. To accomplish that task, they must be striving towards holiness and developing self-control. The fruits of the spirit are those traits that characterize a person who has the Holy Spirit living within them, one most notably being self-control (Eph 5:22–23). Paul continues the importance of self-control by labeling it as one of the few characteristics of a pastor. Why is this? John Macarthur said:

> Self-control is absolutely vital to lasting success in any endeavor of life. Many people do attain a degree of prominence on the strength of sheer natural talent alone. But the real, influential *leaders* are the ones who devote themselves to personal discipline and make the most of their gifts. Those who utterly lack self-control will invariably fail, and they forfeit the example of integrity so essential to the best kind of true leadership.[6]

Those who lack self-control fail to seek after holiness. Those who do not seek after holiness will ultimately fail not only as pastors, but as followers of Christ.

---

5. Whitney, *Spiritual Disciplines for the Christian Life*, 9.

6. MacArthur, *The Book on Leadership*, 146.

THREE DISCIPLINES YOU SHOULD NEVER OVERLOOK

Scripture Reading/Bible Intake

No other spiritual discipline compares in importance to a regular digestion of the word of God. The words of the Bible are the primary tool God uses to communicate to his children. The greatest benefit of Scripture is that it is "profitable for teaching, for reproof, for correction, and for training in righteousness" (2 Tim 3:16, ESV). That is why Paul used his final words to Timothy to command him to "preach the word; be ready in season and out of season; reprove, rebuke, and exhort, with complete patience and teaching" (2 Tim 4:2, ESV). The word of God is the only thing on earth that will truly change lives. As a Christian and church leader, you do not need to be convinced of the importance of Scripture. You preach these words weekly. The most difficult part of Bible intake is what method you will use.

READ DAILY

Every day you should intentionally find the time to read the word of God. The best time for this is typically in the morning. Wake up early before your daily activities and find a quiet place to read. This quiet location may be in your home, in your office, or in your car before you enter into your place of employment. If you are not a morning person, consider reading during your lunch break. The important part is consistency.

READ INTENTIONALLY

The second problem that occurs behind time constraints is what to read. The best way to tackle this problem is by following a reading plan. A reading plan helps you stay focused and on-task. Some avoid reading plans because they seem legalistic, but if used as a guide they assist the reader in consuming the whole counsel of Scripture. Many people are not natural readers, so a plan makes reading the entirety of the Bible achievable. A simple reading plan is to read three chapters every day to finish the Bible in roughly a year. My favorite reading plan has passages from the epistles, the law, history, poetry, psalms, prophecy, and the Gospels over a seven-day period. A plan such as this takes the reader through the Bible in a year but also does not allow the reader to get lost for days in Leviticus and Numbers.

Read purposefully

Remember Bible intake is for devotion, not sermon prep. The greatest problem most preachers have is going to Scripture only for sermon content and not seeking personal life-change from Scripture. In Jerry Vines's book *Power in the Pulpit,* he shared how he struggled with the difference when he was in college:

> I was majoring in Bible, and my days were filled with many, many chapters from the Bible, sometimes thirty nightly . . . I convinced myself I was reading the Bible as much as I needed. I failed to understand there is a difference between reading the Bible to take a test and reading God's Word to feed one's heart . . . As a result of my neglect of daily devotional time, my heart became cold to the things of God . . . On the outside, everything seemed fine. No one would have known I was far from God.[7]

Pastors and church leaders, God wants to use his word to change your heart just like he desires to change the hearts of those you lead. For that to occur, Bible intake for devotion must take place.

Prayer

If Bible intake is God's primary way to speak to us, then prayer is our primary way to communicate with God. Spurgeon told his students, "Of course the preacher is above all others distinguished as a man of prayer. He prays as an ordinary Christian, else he were a hypocrite. He prays more than ordinary Christians, else he were disqualified for the office which he has undertaken."[8] Consider the disciples: one of the few things they asked the Lord to do was to teach them to pray (Luke 11:1). Prayer is by far one of the most important tasks for church leaders to engage in. No moment compares to the moments communing with God in prayer. Prayer has a unique way to humble and encourage every follower of Christ. The model shown throughout Scripture is that God has a unique way to work through

7. Vines and Shaddix, *Power in the Pulpit,* 60.

8. Spurgeon, *Lectures to My Students,* 40.

the prayers of a righteous person (Jas 5:13–16). This reality should change the way we pray.

Pray often and daily

Prayer should take place more often than conversations with your spouse. Paul told the church at Thessalonica to "pray without ceasing" (1 Thess 5:17). In every situation and every moment, our default position should be to pray. At the very least, prayer should be a part of a Christian's daily quiet time. After reading Scripture in the morning five to ten minutes should be solely dedicated to talking to the Lord. At a minimum, pray for direction, for your day, for your family, and allow time for the Lord to respond.

Pray in accordance with the will of God

God desires for us to pray in accordance with his will. On the night before Jesus was arrested he prayed in Gethsemane (Matt 26:39). He prayed that the Lord's will would be done in spite of what it meant for him. Jesus also taught us how to pray for the salvation of individuals (Matt 9:38). In the clearest form, Jesus said to pray, "Your kingdom come, your will be done" (Matt 6:10). Pray in accordance with the will of God.

Pray to battle spiritual warfare

The most notable way that Jesus combatted the attacks of Satan was through prayer. As he went into the wilderness, he was praying. Also, throughout his ministry, Jesus retreated to be with the Father and pray. He taught his disciples to pray. The reality is that we are never more like Jesus than when we pray. As followers of Christ, the best way to combat temptation and spiritual warfare is to be in constant contact with the Father. The enemy is in full force to attack church leaders, so by all means, pray.

Sabbath

Behind Bible intake and prayer, by far the most import spiritual discipline for pastor or church leader is the practice of Sabbath rest. Peter Scazzero, author of *The Emotionally Healthy Leader*, defined biblical Sabbath as "a twenty-four-hour block of time in which we stop work, enjoy rest, practice delight, and contemplate God."[9] Of all the spiritual disciplines, Sabbath is the first modeled in Scripture. When God rested from creation on the seventh day, it was not because God needed rest. He was only modeling rest for his creation.

In the midst of a pastor's busy schedule, stopping to rest seems almost impossible. For smaller-membership church pastors and bivocational ministers, a work week could be anywhere from forty to seventy-five hours a week. Unfortunately, God has commanded his followers to practice Sabbath. When God gave the people of Israel the Ten Commandments, the first command after honoring God and not seeking idols is the command to practice Sabbath. So why Sabbath?

SABBATH IS DESIGNED TO STOP WORK AND ENJOY REST

In our society, the idea to stop and rest seems like a form of laziness. It was a concept I believed in and followed earlier in my ministry. In my last semester of Masters work in seminary, I was faced with the reality that I did not practice Sabbath rest. I was working two secular jobs and serving on staff at a local church. Monday through Friday I bounced between my two part-time jobs. On Saturday, I prepared for church and worked on school work, and Sunday was a full church day. My life was full seven days a week. That lifestyle landed me in the ER. Stress and anxiety had overwhelmed me. I was relying on myself instead of relying on God. Many ministers live their lives the same way. Scazzero said, "Keeping the Sabbath is a core spiritual discipline—an essential delivery mechanism for God's grace and goodness in our lives. It provides a God-ordained way to slow us down for meaningful connection with God, ourselves, and those we care about."[10]

SABBATH REQUIRES INTENTIONALITY

Like every other spiritual discipline, Sabbath requires intentionality. For many pastors, Sabbath may not be a day but parts of two days. Some begin Sabbath on Friday night and rest until Saturday afternoon. Some pick a day

9. Scazzero, *The Emotionally Healthy Leader*, 144.
10. Ibid., 156.

in the middle of the week and take the full day off. At the very least, rest needs to occur twenty-four hours a week.

SABBATH IS DESIGNED FOR WORSHIP

Consider spending the day at the lake or beach. Go for a hike, run, or bike ride in which you marvel at God's creation. Spend the day cutting grass and praying. Enjoy time laughing with your family. Go to a coffee shop and read Scripture for a couple hours. Sabbath is designed to rest in God and enjoy his creation and the many blessings he has given you.

A burned-out, dried-out pastor is useless. A pastor without rest is a pastor who will ultimately find himself useless in ministry. The story is told of a young pastor who said that he would rather burn out in ministry than rust out. Whether a pastor burns out or rusts out, they are still out. Pastors, honor God by practicing Sabbath rest.

CONCLUSION

"You can't lead anyone further than you have gone yourself." One of the reasons Gene Mauch was unable to lead his team to the World Series was because he had never been as a player. It is nearly impossible for a pastor to lead his church further in their relationship with Christ if he has not first sought Christ above all else. Pastors and church leaders, for the sake of your ministry, seek Christ by allowing him to speak to you through his work, communing with him through prayer, and resting in him through Sabbath. Your ministry depends on it.

BIBLIOGRAPHY

MacArthur, John. *The Book on Leadership: The Power of a Godly Influence*. Nashville: Thomas Nelson, 2004.

Norcross John, "Auld Lang Syne: Success predictors, change processes, and self-reported outcomes of New Year's resolvers and nonresolvers." *Journal of Clinical Psychology* 58, no. 4 (2002): 397–405.

Scazzero, Peter. *The Emotionally Healthy Leader: How Transforming Your Inner Life Will Deeply Transform Your Church, Team, and the World*. Grand Rapids: Zondervan, 2015.

Spurgeon, Charles. *Lectures to My Students*. Pasadena, TX: Pilgrim, 1990.

Vines, Jerry, and Jim Shaddix. *Power in the Pulpit: How to Prepare and Deliver Expository Sermons*. Chicago: Moody, 1999.

Whitney, Donald S. *Spiritual Disciplines for the Christian Life*, revised and updated ed. Colorado Springs, CO: NavPress, 2014.

Willard, Dallas. *The Spirit of the Disciplines: Understanding How God Changes Lives*. San Francisco: Harper & Row, 1988.

10

The Pastor's Family Life
in the Small Church

Mark Tolbert

The role of the family is crucial in the life and ministry of the pastor. Like those in other callings or careers, ministers are expected to perform their duties with excellence. Unlike some other callings, however, the pastor must also exercise his calling out of his godly character. Competency alone is not enough. I know of few ministers that fail due to a competency issue; many that stumble do so due to flaws in their character. The main proving ground and arena for a minister's character is in his family life. Family is the laboratory where our faith is on display. For the minister of the gospel, how one functions in his family is most important.

Why is family so crucial for one called to ministry? What are the factors to consider in assessing the health of your family as they impact your ministry? In this chapter, we will consider four facets of family as they relate to the health and effectiveness of your ministry. As a diamond is rated in the four facets of carat, color, clarity, and cut, we will examine the status and health of our families as we consider the platform, priority, problems, and passion of the ministry family.

A PLATFORM FOR MINISTRY

What is a platform? The dictionary defines a platform as: "(noun) 1. a horizontal surface or structure with a horizontal surface raised above the level of the surrounding area. 2. a raised flooring or other horizontal surface, such as, in a hall or meeting place, a stage for use by public speakers, performers, etc."[1] While the dictionary makes a platform synonymous with a stage, I believe there is an important distinction.

At New Orleans Baptist Theological Seminary, we teach our students that the area at the front of the worship center is to be called the platform, not the stage. We insist that there is a significant difference in the two terms. A stage is for performance; a platform is for influence. We do not want to produce preachers and worship leaders that perform ministry as a stage performance. There is an element of pretense and hypocrisy in mere performance. We want to foster ministers who preach and lead music out of their own authentic worship, leading others to follow their example. These ministers see the elevated section as a platform, raised to a level to be seen not for performance but for influence.

There is a virtual platform from which we do ministry, and that is our character. Pastors, like professors, plumbers, and painters, are expected to be competent in their skills, diligent in their labor and committed to excellence in their work. The people that mow yards, repair engines, perform surgery, and shepherd God's people should take pride in their work, strive to do their best and be deserving of their wages. These should be universal standards and expectations.

The role of the pastor, however, has a unique requirement: the success of the pastor's work is uniquely tethered to his character. This is a component of pastoral ministry that, if not entirely unique, is uncommon for other callings or professions. The mechanic may be able to fix the most difficult and broken mechanical problem and yet have broken relationships and issues in his life. The best-selling author may be able to weave a compelling storyline and sell millions of books, but the storyline of his life could be a tragic tale of hypocrisy and scandal. These character issues are not necessarily disqualifying for some professions. This is not the case for the pastor.

The one called to serve as a pastor is required to serve out of his character as well as his competence. Every shepherd since David has been expected to flesh out the description of Psalm 78:72: "So he shepherded them

---

1. *Definithing*, https://definithing.com/define-dictionary/platform/.

according to the integrity of his heart, and guided them with his skillful hands" (NASB). The integrity of the pastor's life is the foundation upon which ministry function and pastoral duties are performed successfully.

Perhaps the most visible platform of our character is our family life. Home is where life is lived out in all of its reality. Family is where defenses are lowered and the real you comes through. That is why the Psalmist determined, "I will give heed to the blameless way. When will you come to me? I will walk within my house in the integrity of my heart" (Ps 101:2, NASB). Your home is a platform where life is on display.

Ministry has been defined as "fishbowl living." This is particularly true when the pastor lives in a parsonage or a pastorium. Church members know where you live, if your car is in the driveway, and whether you keep your lights on and your lawn mowed. Even if you do not live in church-owned property, ministry can be very much like life in a fishbowl. Most of the time, this description has a negative connotation. Certainly, being on continual display can be intimidating. Who in their right mind would want everyone always watching everything they do? That is why the whole idea of fishbowl living is generally viewed as a horrible burden.

But there is a flipside to the concept of fishbowl living. Recognizing the visibility of the pastor's home is reality. That is why James 3:1 observes, "Let not many of you become teachers, my brethren, knowing that as such we will incur a stricter judgment" (NASB). Although it may not seem fair, it is reality that we are being watched and judged more strictly than other people. This reality, however, also affords the pastor's family the opportunity to be on full display for others to observe the reality of their walk with Christ.

Since the pastor's home is so visible, why not leverage that as a platform for authentic ministry? For the minister that truly desires to lead his family in following the Lord, the family's commitment to Christ is a powerful platform which undergirds all aspects of ministry. The preaching, pastoral care, counseling, and other formal ministries are verified by the informal platform of the pastor's indisputable family life.

Scripture records both positive and negative examples of ministry that is supported or sabotaged by its family foundation. Positive family examples abound throughout Scripture. Children in Scripture are influenced to follow the Lord because of the influence of godly parents. Hannah dedicated her son, Samuel to the Lord (1 Sam 1:28). Timothy was blessed by the examples of a godly mother and a godly grandmother (2 Tim 1:5).

Husband-and-wife teams like Priscilla and Aquila ministered to the Lord together (Acts 18:18).

Negative examples of toxic families are also recorded in Scripture. King Saul's jealousy toward David is clearly seen in his hatred of his own son, Jonathan, because of the son's friendship with David. In 1 Samuel 20:30 it says, "Then Saul's anger burned against Jonathan and he said to him, 'You son of a perverse, rebellious woman! Do I not know that you are choosing the son of Jesse to your own shame and to the shame of your mother's nakedness?'" (NASB). The priest Eli's ministry was compromised because of his undisciplined sons: "Now the sons of Eli were worthless men; they did not know the LORD" (1 Sam 2:12, NASB). Famously, David, in spite of having a heart for God, severely damaged his reputation, his family, and his legacy by his moral failure with Bathsheba.

When your family is a clear reflection of your public ministry it is a powerful platform from which to build. The way you relate to your spouse, your children and your parents underscores and magnifies your sermons, worship leadership, and youth ministry. When your family interaction falls short of the biblical standard, your public ministry can be compromised. Although no family is perfect, it must be genuine and sincere. If your family life is one of pretense and hypocrisy, your public ministry can be nothing more than a stiff performance, an acting job on display upon a stage, not a platform. Platform alone is not ministry. There must be competency, and faithfulness. Ministry can parallel much as when a performer takes the stage, but it is the platform from which one then can perform authentic ministry.

A PRIORITY OF MINISTRY

When I was called to my first church as pastor, I told the leadership that my family would come before my ministry. I was excited about being called as their pastor. Although I had more than eight years of prior ministry experience, this would be my first assignment as senior pastor. I wanted to do a good job! However, I wanted the leadership to know of the priority of my family, hence I gave them my perspective that my family came ahead of my ministry. After several months, I was feeling the competition, often in my own mind, for my time and attention. Would it go to my family or to my ministry? I felt conflicted and guilty, whichever choice I made. When with my family, I felt I may be neglecting my ministry; when engaged in ministry, I wondered if I was neglecting my family. My family and my ministry seemed to be in direct competition with each other! How could I possibly resolve the tension?

Family and ministry are not to be pitted against one another. It is not that your family comes before your ministry. It is certainly not that your ministry comes before your family. From a biblical standpoint, your family is actually your first and foremost ministry; family is your ministry priority. According to the Pastoral Epistles, a man is only qualified for the pastoral office if he meets the conditions set forth in Scripture. These conditions include family priorities such as devotion to one's wife and managing one's children (2 Tim 3:2–4). The clear implication is that one must function *first* in one's household before expanding one's sphere of influence. If a man fails to function in his family context he is disqualified from further responsibilities.

The clear force of Scripture suggests that rather than family coming before one's ministry, one's ministry in and to the family is one's first, primary ministry. Not only is family the platform for ministry, the family is the launch pad for ministry. Husbands are to start with their wife (Eph 5:25–26) and children (Eph 6:4) and minister to them first. In setting the priority of the family, the pastor has a basis for further ministry. The family is the laboratory where ministry skills are learned and honed. Seeing the family as one's first ministry is not only biblical, it will also relieve the pastor of some degree of false guilt when devoting time and energy to his family.

FACING PROBLEMS IN MINISTRY

When sensing the call to ministry, the response and responsibility of the family can be a major source of conflict in ministry. How will my family respond to me sensing a call to ministry? What part will your family play in the ministry to which you feel called? If you are married, what will be the role of your wife? If you have children, how will you set expectations for the children? If you have parents, and we all do or did at one time, what about their response to your decision to become a minister of the gospel?

Not all ministers come from families that appreciate the significance of a call to ministry. When I entered college, I chose Biology as my major. I did so as a result of my desire to go on to dental school and enter the dental profession. God interrupted my plans during the summer between my junior and senior year of college. He called me to ministry, a call that displeased my parents, especially my father. I remember the kitchen table conversation I had with my dad, when I laid before him what I sensed God was calling me to do. Imagine my disappointment when his reply was, "Well, I think you are throwing your life away."

I was devastated! Everyone longs for the blessing of their mother and father. For my father to see my decision as a wasted life was shattering to me. I was heartbroken that he would not be rejoicing in his son answering God's call. I am happy to say that he changed his opinion several years later when he came to faith in Christ. He became one of my biggest supporters and cheerleaders. The reality is, however, what he said to me, "you are throwing your life away," had the ring of truth to it. Jesus had actually made this clear when he said, "If anyone comes to me, and does not hate his own father and mother and wife and children and brothers and sisters, yes, and even his own life, he cannot be my disciple" (Luke 14:26). Obviously, my father had a far different intention than did the Lord when he made this statement. God demonstrated to me out of my own experience that when one decides to follow Jesus and answer the Lord's call to ministry, one is in effect, "throwing his life away" for a new life in Jesus Christ.

I was forced to discover that my call to ministry required balancing competing priorities, especially in regards to family life. I had to deal with this in answering God's call versus achieving the blessing of my father. Like most people, particularly men, I longed for my father's blessing. I suspect that desire is hard-wired into men; we want our father to be proud of us, to affirm our choices and decisions and to give us their blessing (Gen 27:36). As I have talked with countless men, I have discovered I am not unique in my need for the blessing of my father. I have also discovered I am not unique in having my call met with less than ecstasy by my parents.

Perhaps some of you were saddened that your family did not welcome your call to ministry with open arms. For those who come from a ministry family, or were encouraged to consider ministry as a calling, many more perhaps answered God's call in the face of surprise, shock, bewilderment, or even opposition. Even Jesus Christ had family members who misunderstood his calling until later in his ministry (Matt 12:46–50). The possibility of following God's call in the face of family disapproval is a real and often painful reality for a pastor. God encourages us to live our lives in obedience to him and his call, and to trust him as we navigate relational waters with our families, especially with parents and siblings.

Following Jesus requires leaving, while loving, one's family. That can be very tricky! Scripture is clear that the call to follow Jesus requires a readiness to leave the parents we love and honor. Matthew 19:19 records Jesus' reminder to "honor your father and mother" and just ten verses later in Matthew 19:29, our Lord reminds us that those who have "left houses or brothers or sisters or father or mother or children or farms for my name's sake, will receive many times as much, and will inherit eternal life." Just because one loves his parents does not relieve one of the duty to leave said parents. On the other hand, when one chooses to be prepared to leave one's parents (in the biblical sense) does not relieve one of the command to honor one's parents. Many, if not most Christians, especially ministers, will need to balance these competing yet complementary injunctions to love and leave.

What about the ongoing role of family in ministry? Once you leave home and your parents, it is often only a matter of time until your family takes on a new identity. Unless a pastor remains single, ministers typically marry and have children of their own. Then the role of family is a new issue of wife and children and church, in that order.

Consideration of your spouse in following God's will is essential. My situation is somewhat unique in that Joy surrendered to a call in her life before I did. Joy and I were high-school sweethearts. We came to Christ as a result of attending a Billy Graham movie at a local theater in Atlanta, Georgia. She attended a conference the summer following her high school graduation. At the close of the conference, Dr. Bill Bright issued a challenge "to go anywhere and do anything to help fulfill the Great Commission of our Lord." She surrendered to that challenge. We married after my freshman year of college, and began to pursue our majors. For me it was a degree in Biology and then on to dental school.

During the summer between my junior and senior years in college, we attended Explo 72 in Dallas, Texas. An international congress on evangelism, Explo 72 was a historic gathering of 80,000 high school and college students. The final night of the conference was a mass rally in the Cotton Bowl Stadium. At the closing ceremony, a remarkable thing happened: Dr. Bill Bright issued a challenge "to go anywhere and do anything to help fulfill the Great Commission of our Lord." I made the same commitment that Joy had made four years earlier.

Over the next six months, I struggled to interpret what the Lord was directing me to do. During that process, I asked my wife, Joy, "How would you feel if the Lord was directing us toward ministry?" Her incredible response was, "Whatever God shows you to do, I will follow you." As a result, she was all-in when I finally surrendered to God's call on my life. This is, obviously, the ideal and easiest scenario for a ministry couple. Both the husband and wife each have sensed a divine call to be involved in vocational ministry. Their individual calls merge in their marriage as they serve the Lord together, yet each out of their personal call and surrender to ministry.

The way in which your spouse responds to God's call on your life may vary. Some wives may have experienced a personal call that fully complements and parallels your call. This is perhaps ideal, but may also be somewhat rare. Others may sense a call to support you, whatever he calls you to do. This is perhaps the most common situation. With many ministry couples, the wife wants to encourage, support, and walk alongside her husband as he follows the Lord. It is not that she necessarily feels a call to vocational ministry; she simply wants to follow her husband! This is a common and workable situation. The key here is mutual respect and appreciation from both minister and mate. The minister should express gratitude for the mate that trusts the minister to follow God's call to ministry and show full support and joy in serving with him. The mate should express appreciation to the minister/husband for surrendering to follow the Lord's call, and respect for having a husband that leads her as he follows the Lord.

The most challenging scenario for a ministry couple is when the minister's wife does not support the husband in answering God's call. This is a real and not uncommon problem. I have encountered several men who faced the challenge of not receiving support from their wife. What should one do in this situation? Let me be direct: I would not encourage a man to proceed with pursuing vocational ministry without receiving the blessing and support of his wife. Several reasons drive me to this conviction. First, the primary ministry to which one is called is family; one cannot be considered a successful minister in a church if one neglects to lead one's family. The Pastoral Epistles list the qualifications of a pastor, which include family priorities (1 Tim 3:2–4; Titus 1:6). Second, the minister will never be successful in a church setting without the support and assistance of his family, especially his wife. Ministry is stressful, and the minister needs the support, encouragement, and refuge of a safe and happy home. Third, the model of a happy family is the foundation from which all other ministry is built. Family does not come before your ministry; family is your first ministry! You do not stop there, but you start there. You can do more ministry than just ministry to your family, and you should. However, you cannot do any real effective, long-lasting ministry unless you have ministered first and foremost to your family.

The important role of your wife continues throughout your lifetime of answering God's call to ministry. What input, if any, should your wife have as you consider new and changing ministry assignments? Once again, she should be consulted throughout the process. When you are asked to accept a call to a church or other ministry location, you should seek the prayers and thoughts of your spouse. Such a move usually requires moving to a new location. Obviously, she will be leaving friends, family, familiarity, and often her job in order to support you. The decision to accept a new ministry should be a joint decision between the minister and his wife.

What role should children play in the decision to move to a new ministry assignment? The answer depends upon the age or particular needs of the children. In most cases, younger children will simply be informed of the decision. They need to hear that Mommy and Daddy are following God's call upon their family. Older children or teenagers will need to be included a bit more in the decision. Special family circumstances may present challenges that need to be considered, including whether or not to move during teenage years, or disrupt educational needs or medical needs, among others. Although the decision to move may be hard, they need to understand that they need to trust their parents to trust the Lord. Following the Lord is not always easy; sometimes it proves to be difficult. Children can learn a valuable life lesson as they see the family trust and obey as God calls.

When coming to a new ministry, what should be the expectations upon a minister's family? This is one of the most crucial and significant issues facing a minister and his family. It is not unusual for a pastor search committee to address this issue during the interview process. Sometimes in an indirect way and other times directly, a search committee will raise questions or issues related to the role of the family, especially the wife and children and their roles and expectations before the church family. These issues need to be addressed during the interview process, or in the very earliest phases of the new pastor's ministry at the latest.

The minister should be very intentional about setting expectations for the church concerning the role of his wife and children. It should be obvious that the minister's family should be an example to the church concerning a dedicated Christian family. That is what we have been discussing throughout this chapter. However, church expectations for the pastor's family must be reasonable expectations. These expectations should not be artificial ideas that have been randomly determined by certain influential members. Neither should these expectations be a reaction to perceived strengths or weaknesses of previous pastors' families.

Just as they may do with pastoral expectations, committee members may unfairly compare the previous pastor's family with the new family. These expectations may include the behavior of the children, involvement in various church activities, and involvement of the wife in ministry functions. If the previous family was perceived in a certain way, these perceptions may be automatically imposed upon the new family. A wife may be expected to play the piano, sing specials, and teach Bible studies, or any of a multitude of ministries, because the previous pastor's wife did, or in some cases, did not perform these tasks. Similarly, the pastor's children may be expected to live up to random expectations that are expressed or assumed by the committee and the church. The list of expectations may very well include whether or not the wife works outside of the home, how many children the family plans to have, how they plan to educate their children (public, private, or homeschool education), etc.

How does a minister navigate such expectations? The answer is, by clearly and intentionally setting expectations and boundaries at the outset. The pastor and his family should be an example of a family that loves Jesus, has surrendered to the Lord, and exercises their unique set of spiritual gifts and passions. The wife of the pastor should be an example of a spirit-filled wife—period! The pastor should make clear that his wife will not be "David trying to wear Saul's armor." She will exercise her God-given talents and gifts in serving through the church. The children will be guided by their parents to love, follow, and serve Jesus as the parents decide is in the best interests of the child.

In my family we sought to follow these guidelines. My wife is a godly woman who loves the Lord, exercises her spiritual gift of mercy, teaches the Bible to children and women, and shares her faith in Christ. She sometimes sings in the choir, goes on mission trips, counsels other women, and visits the sick. She does not sing specials, play the piano, serve on committees, or lead the Women's Ministry, as these are not her gifts or passions. My children were required to attend worship services, Youth Bible study, and Wednesday night activities. All other youth activities were optional and were left to their discretion, especially when they were teenagers. My wife and I were thrilled that they generally chose to participate in all youth activities, but not because the church expected it or their parents required it. They did so because of their love for Jesus.

This brings up a critical issue for consideration. I would urge ministers to exercise care when guiding the family concerning guidelines for what the family chooses to do or not do. Specifically, "Why do we do this?" Or, "Why do we not do that?" As much as possible, let the standard be: "We do what we do because we love Jesus." I would suggest caution in saying, "We do what we do because we are in the ministry. We cannot do something because Daddy is the preacher. We must do this because the church expects us to do so." I find these kind of statements filled with serious dangers. For one thing, toddlers and teenagers do not consider themselves "called to ministry." Daddy may be called, but seven-year-old Tommy is not. To impose a blanket of ministerial duty on children poses a serious potential for resentment and rebellion. It runs the risk of infusing your children with a real hostility toward the ministry and the church because they are denied their desires out of an artificial and unfair standard that was not of their choosing—a call to ministry.

On the other hand, the pastor and his wife should have high standards of conduct and behavior. They should hold to clear biblical convictions that drive their behavior, including their entertainment, friends, recreation, and lifestyle. The rationale for the family's choices however is not generally, the fact that they are in the ministry. Rather, the standard is that we do these things and choose not to do other things, because we love and follow Jesus. My wife and I tried to follow that standard. I do not remember telling my children that we did not do something because "Daddy is the preacher." We avoided saying we had to do something, because the church expected it. We sought to instill in our children the motivation of deciding what to do because we love the Lord.

Another common pitfall is the danger of using your family as sermon illustrations. When preaching sermons, vivid illustrations can shed light upon biblical truth. A readily available stockpile of living illustrations comes from the pastor's family life. Cute things said or done by little Suzy or Billy can easily find their way into the pastor's sermons. Please, be careful. Family illustrations should be used very sparingly. Two considerations come into play here: the interests of the church and the privacy of the family. The pastor should realize that the comments and behavior of Suzy and Bobby are simply not as cute to everyone else as they are to the pastor. Do not bore the congregation with incessant stories of your children or grandchildren! Also, respect the privacy of your family. Do not embarrass them with stories they do not want shared. As a rule, do not use your wife or children as sermon illustrations without their permission. Check with them in advance, and make sure they are comfortable with being used as an illustration in your sermon. Use both of these balancing checkpoints before using your family to spice up your sermon.

Ministry can be woven together with family time. We would often attend conferences and conventions as a family. Ministers are sometimes expected to attend denominational events and meetings. These were usually held at a distance from where we lived. These obligations would sometimes prove to be a mixed bag; I had to attend a meeting at a location that I had always wanted to visit. After the business sessions and meetings were completed, we would attempt to schedule family vacation or retreat time. The Tolbert family enjoyed these trips, many of which allowed us to visit places we otherwise might not get to go. Our children—now grown—have told us those are some of their happiest childhood memories.

Ministry can sometimes be a family affair on the church field. Having church members and prospects into the home for dinner can be the doorway to new friendships. Church camps and activities can be fun times for the pastor's family. In my case, I found opportunities to make pastoral visitation a family affair. My son enjoyed making pastoral visits with me on Saturdays. Jason and I would make the needed Saturday visits and end with a stop for ice cream. On one occasion, my son and I visited a lost man at his home, discovering that he had a son about the same age as my son. A few Sundays after our visit, the man came to faith in Christ. In his testimony, he said that during our visit, he saw in me and Jason a picture of a Christian father, and wanted to be a Christian father to his son. As a young boy, my son was excited that he had a part in this man coming to faith in Jesus. That man, now with the Lord, pointed to the impact of our family witness, as a strong motivating factor in his coming to faith.

I have had a number of ministers serve as models and encouragers throughout my ministry. I have also had bitter disappointments due to the failure of fellow ministers, some of whom were close personal friends. The man who mentored me when I was a new Christian later abandoned his wife and left the faith. Two of my closest ministry colleagues, both of whom had preached in churches where I was the pastor, had stinging moral failures, including unfaithfulness to their wives. It is tragic when long years of effective ministry can be sabotaged by an oversight of the priority of marriage. Be aware of the significance and importance of your family. Satan aims his biggest guns on God's servants. The damage to your ministry cannot be overstated. Protect your marriage. Place guards in place to avoid the darts of the enemy. Your family is a big deal!

In spite of everything you may do, your family will likely make sacrifices and even become the casualties of ministry. My grown children tell me that when they were teenagers they worried that if they misbehaved, their daddy would lose his job. My wife has been dearly loved by the vast majority of our church members, but she has also on occasion been hurt and betrayed by close friends. Such are the pitfalls of ministry.

The difficult moments of ministry are sometimes used by God for his purposes. A very difficult family experience, where our family was deeply hurt by a church member's actions, proved to be used for good. The details are too personal to relate. I am able to share that the painful experience our family endured resulted in a member of the community coming to faith in Christ. The word came back to us that our family's response to being mistreated was a witness to the grace of God that caused an onlooker to want the same Jesus he saw in our family. That person is now in glory. Praise the Lord!

A PASSION FOR MINISTRY

The love of family members for each other and their love for the Lord should empower the pastor and his family through the adventure of ministry. Ministry can be messy. It can also be rewarding. We need to love our wife well, not just because we are in ministry but because we love the Lord and are grateful for his gift of a helpmate. We need to love our children well and teach them to love the Lord, not because they are preacher's kids, but because the Lord loves us and we should love him in return. Our children are now grown with children of their own. My wife and I pray that we have given them roots and wings. Roots are what you give them while they are young. Wings are what they will need as you release them to follow their dreams.

One of the most affirming moments of ministry for me came as a result of a church member's observation of my marriage. I was a pastor in Little Rock, Arkansas. One of our members had taken on a project to recognize all of the pastors that had served our church over the years. She had painstakingly collected photographs of each pastor, had them matted and framed and selected a specific location in the church fellowship hall to display them. She had done a great job and it proved to be a real blessing to the church family.

The week of the scheduled display, Ira asked me to preview the display of pastor photographs. She began with the photograph of the first pastor of the church. She explained that he served before she came along, but described his ministry in glowing terms, specifically highlighting one of his exceptional ministry skills. She moved to the next photograph, once again speaking in praise of his particular pastoral competency. The third pastor was one whom she knew personally and she followed in the same pattern, concentrating on this man's strength in ministry. As she moved along, she described each pastor in a positive and very specific way. Finally she arrived at the current pastor's picture, and she said, "And now you are our pastor, and you are the best we have ever had." "Oh, no," I replied. "You said something specific about all of these others. I need to know what you will say about my ministry someday." "That's easy," she said. "You love your wife more than any pastor we have ever had." I was stunned, humbled and pleased. I decided that was high praise indeed. As much as I want to be a good preacher, evangelist, leader, administrator, and all of the other parts involved in pastoral ministry, I would be delighted to be remembered for my love and ministry to my family. I do not know that I deserve such praise, but I was thrilled to be offered it.

As a long-time pastor, and now seminary professor, I am able to look back upon the joys and sorrows of the merging of ministry and family. Both of our grown children love the Lord and serve him, one at a Christian University and the other in a Christian high school. My oldest grandson is studying at a Christian University and is praying about what God is calling him to do. I officiated at both of my childrens' wedding ceremonies. I have had the joy of baptizing parents, children, and grandchildren. I would like to believe that my family has been blessed because we have sought to answer his call and follow the Lord. That is not to say that it has always been easy. The will of God is not always easy. The will of God is not always a safe place to be; but the will of God is always the sweetest place to be. Is following the Lord easy? No. Is the risk to your family a factor? Of course, but so is the reward. Consider carefully the impact on your family in answering God's call to ministry. Jesus said we are to count the cost. The cost in following the Lord may be high; the cost in not following the Lord will be higher.

Conclusion

Jeffrey Farmer

"Whatever you do in word or deed, do all in the name of the Lord Jesus, giving thanks through him to God the Father" (Col 3:17, NASB). Paul's instruction to the church in Colossae included this wonderful summary of Colossians 3:12–16. The simplest understanding of this verse is to consider everything you say or do as an act of worship. How we live our lives reflects how we view Jesus Christ. If our work is shoddy, then we communicate disrespect for the King of kings. If we truly value our Savior, we will do our very best. He is truly worthy of our best. In short, we should conduct our lives and our ministries with excellence.

It should be noted that excellence does not necessarily mean perfection. Too many confuse the two and, finding themselves unable to live perfect lives, abandon the pursuit altogether. Instead, we must live excellent lives. We are to live each day saying and doing the very best we are able to do.

The key to excellence in ministry is intentionality. Just as no one drifts toward evangelism, no one conducts their ministry with excellence casually. It is an intentional decision each morning. Before getting out of bed, the believer's first prayer should be that God will give him/her the strength to give his/her absolute best all day. The believer should offer his/her actions as a living sacrifice. The pastor should model this to the congregation.

SOME ADVICE FROM THE FIELD

I regularly have the opportunity to talk with seasoned, smaller-membership church pastors. Recently, I asked a number of them to share some advice for new pastors serving in smaller churches. Among the first responses were "Learn from the very beginning what it means to be a small-church pastor. Focus right on the beginning to accentuate the strengths, to recognize the weaknesses, and fix where possible. Be okay with being a small-church pastor." It is very helpful for your mental well-being for you to understand that you are not a megachurch pastor. You do not have the resources of a megachurch (or even a large church), and so your expectations should reflect this fact. As another pastor commented, "Pray more. Work faithfully, and expect less. I don't mean lowering God's standard, but I do mean that I would expect fewer dramatic changes when taking over a long-established church. I thought I could really teach them something to inspire the congregation and community, but really it was I who had the most to learn."

In this book, we have endeavored to provide the tools necessary to conduct your ministry with excellence. We want you to be successful in your ministry because of who you work for. Remember that you are not pastoring a church so that you can make a living. There are plenty of jobs out there for that. You are not pastoring a church for celebrity or for recognition. You are pastoring because God has called you to serve him. Your reward will be to hear him say, "Well done, good and faithful servant" (Matt 25:21), and that will be reward enough!

APPENDIX A

Resources by Chapter

CHAPTER 4

Selected Bibliography for Sermon Preparation

Adams, Jay E. *Sermon Analysis: A Preacher's Personal Improvement Textbook and Workbook*. Denver: Accent, 1986.

Akin, Daniel L., et al. *Engaging Exposition*. Nashville: B&H Academic, 2011.

Arthurs, Jeffery. *Preaching with Variety*. Grand Rapids: Kregel, 2007.

Baumann, J. Daniel. *An Introduction to Contemporary Preaching*. Grand Rapids: Baker, 1973.

Blackwood, Andrew W. *The Preparation of Sermons*. New York: Abingdon-Cokesbury, 1948.

Broadus, John A. *On the Preparation and Delivery of Sermons*. 4th ed. Revised and edited by Vernon L. Stanfield. San Francisco: Harper & Row, 1979.

Brown, H. C. Jr., et al. *Steps to the Sermon, Revised*. Nashville: Broadman and Holman, 1996.

Bryson, Harold. *Expository Preaching*. Nashville: Broadman and Holman, 1995.

Bryson, Harold T., and James E. Taylor. *Building Sermons to Meet People's Needs*. Nashville: Broadman, 1980.

Carter, Terry, et al. *Preaching God's Word*. Grand Rapids: Zondervan, 2005.

Chapell, Bryan. *Christ-Centered Preaching*. 2d ed. Grand Rapids: Baker, 2005.

———. "The Future of Expository Preaching." *Preaching Magazine* 20 (September-October, 2004) 42–43.

Charles, H.B. Jr. *On Preaching: Personal & Pastoral Insights for the Preparation & Practice of Preaching*. Chicago: Moody, 2014.

Cothen, Joe H. *The Pulpit is Waiting: A Guide for Pastoral Preaching*. Gretna, LA: Pelican, 1998.

Davis, H. Grady. *Design for Preaching*. Philadelphia: Muhlenberg, 1958.

Dever, Mark, and Greg Gilbert. *Preach: Theology Meets Practice*. Nashville: B & H Academic, 2012.

167

APPENDIX A: RESOURCES BY CHAPTER

Eslinger, Richard L. *A New Hearing: Living Options in Homiletic Method*. Nashville: Abingdon, 1987.

Fabarez, Michael. *Preaching that Changes Lives*. Nashville: Thomas Nelson, 2002.

Fasol, Al. *Essentials for Biblical Preaching: An Introduction to Basic Sermon Preparation*. Grand Rapids: Baker, 1989.

Faw, Chalmer. *A Guide to Biblical Preaching*. Nashville: Broadman, 1962.

Gibson, Scott M. *Preaching for Special Services*. Grand Rapids: Baker, 2001.

Hall, E. Eugene, and James L. Heflin. *Proclaim the Word: The Bases of Preaching*. Nashville: Broadman, 1985.

Hamilton, Donald L. *Homiletical Handbook*. Nashville: Broadman, 1992.

Heisler, Greg. *Spirit-Led Preaching*. Nashville: Broadman, 2007.

Jones, Ilion T. *Principles and Practice of Preaching*. Nashville: Abingdon, 1956.

Killinger, John. *Fundamentals of Preaching*. Philadelphia: Fortress, 1985.

Larsen, David L. *The Anatomy of Preaching*. Grand Rapids: Baker Book House, 1989.

———. *Telling the Old, Old Story: The Art of Narrative Preaching*. Wheaton, IL: Crossway, 1995.

Lenski, R. C. H. *The Sermon: Its Homiletical Construction*. Reprint. Grand Rapids: Baker, 1968.

Lowry, Eugene L. *The Homiletical Plot: The Sermon as a Narrative Art Form*. Atlanta: John Knox, 1980.

———. *The Sermon: Dancing the Edge of Mystery*. Nashville: Abingdon, 1997.

Luccock, Halford E. *In the Minister's Workshop*. Nashville: Abingdon-Cokesbury, 1944.

MacArthur, John Jr. *Rediscovering Expository Preaching*. Richard L. Mayhue, ed. Dallas: Word, 1992.

MacCartney, Clarence E. *Preaching Without Notes*. New York: Abingdon, 1946.

MacPherson, Ian. *The Art of Illustrating Sermons*. New York: Abingdon, 1964.

Massey, James Earl. *Designing the Sermon: Order and Movement in Preaching*. Nashville: Abingdon, 1980.

McDill, Wayne V. *The Twelve Essential Skills for Great Preaching*. 2d ed. Nashville: B&H Academic, 2006.

Merida, Tony. *Faithful Preaching*. Nashville: B&H Academic, 2009.

Meyer, F. B. *Expository Preaching: Plans and Methods*. Reprint. Grand Rapids: Baker, 1974.

Miller, Donald. *The Way to Biblical Preaching*. New York: Abingdon, 1957.

Olford, Stephen F., and David L. Olford. *Anointed Expository Preaching*. Nashville: Broadman & Holman, 1998.

Pattison, T. H. *The Making of the Sermon*. Philadelphia: American Baptist Publication Society, 1960.

Perry, Lloyd. *Biblical Preaching for Today's World*. Chicago: Moody, 1973.

Pitt-Watson, Ian. *A Primer for Preachers*. Grand Rapids: Baker, 1986.

Robinson, Haddon W. *Biblical Preaching: The Development and Delivery of Expository Messages*. Grand Rapids: Baker, 1980.

Rummage, Stephen N. *Planning Your Preaching: A Step-By-Step Guide for Developing a One-Year Preaching Calendar*. Grand Rapids: Kregel, 2002.

Sangster, W. E. *The Craft of Sermon Construction*. London: Epworth, 1949.

Scharf, Greg. *Prepared to Preach: God's Work and Ours in Proclaiming His Word*. Glasgow: Bell and Bain, 2005.

Stevenson, Dwight E. *In the Biblical Preacher's Workshop*. Nashville: Abingdon, 1967.

Thompson, William. *Preaching Biblically*. New York: Abingdon, 1981.

Vines, Jerry. *A Practical Guide to Sermon Preparation.* Chicago: Moody, 1985.

Vines, Jerry, and Jim Shaddix. *Power in the Pulpit: How to Prepare and Deliver Expository Sermons.* Chicago: Moody, 1999.

Wardlaw, Don M., ed. *Preaching Biblically: Creating Sermons in the Shape of Scripture.* Philadelphia: Westminster, 1983.

Wiersbe, Warren W. *The Dynamics of Preaching.* Grand Rapids: Baker, 1999.

Willhite, Keith, and Scott M. Gibson, eds. *The Big Idea of Biblical Preaching.* Grand Rapids: Baker, 1998.

York, Herschel W., and Bert Decker. *Preaching with Bold Assurance: A Solid and Enduring Approach to Engaging Exposition.* Nashville: Broadman and Holman, 2003.

CHAPTER 5

For Specific Resources in the Area of Biblical and Theological Foundations of Worship:

Dawn, Marva J. *Reaching Out without Dumbing Down: A Theology of Worship for the Turn-of-the-Century Culture.* Grand Rapids: Wm. B. Eerdmans Publishing Co., 1995.

Harland, Mike, and Stan Moser. *Seven Words of Worship: The Key to a Lifetime of Experiencing God.* Nashville: Broadman and Holman, 2008.

Segler, Franklin M., and Randall Bradley. *Christian Worship: Its Theology and Practice,* 3rd ed. Nashville: Broadman and Holman, 2006.

Sharp, Michael, and Argile Smith. *Holy Gatherings: A Leader's Guide for Engaging the Congregation in Corporate Worship.* Denver: Outskirts, 2009.

Steele, Ed. *Worship HeartCries: Personal Preparation for Corporate Worship,* 2nd ed. Self-published, CreateSpace, 2016.

For Specific Resources in Worship Planning:

Cherry, Constance. *The Music Architect: A Blueprint for Designing Culturally Relevant and Biblically Faithful Services.* Grand Rapids, Baker Academic, 2016.

———. *The Worship Architect: A Blueprint for Designing Culturally Relevant and Biblically Faithful Services.* Grand Rapids, Baker Academic, 2010.

Hicks, Zac. *The Worship Pastor: A Call to Ministry for Worship Leaders and Teams.* Grand Rapids: Zondervan, 2016.

Kauflin, Bob. *Worship Matters: Leading Others to Encounter the Greatness of God.* Wheaton, IL: Crossway, 2008.

Scazzero, Peter. *The Emotionally Healthy Leader: How Transforming Your Inner Life Will Deeply Transform Your Church, Team, and the World.* Grand Rapids: Zondervan, 2015.

For Specific Resources for Worship Leadership:

Bowersox, Steve. *The Worship Musician's Theory Book* Jacksonville: The Bowersox Institute of Music, 1997.

Bradley, Randall. *From Postlude to Prelude: Music Ministry's Other Six Days*. Fenton, MO: Morning Star Music, 2004.

Clark, Paul. *Tune My Heart to Sing Thy Grace: Worship Renewal through Congregational Singin*. Nashville: Crossbooks, 2010.

Noland, Rory. *The Heart of the Artist*. Grand Rapids: Zondervan, 1999.

———. *The Worshiping Artist: Equipping You and Your Ministry Team to Lead Others in Worship*. Grand Rapids: Zondervan, 2007.

Segler, Franklin M., and Randall Bradley. *Christian Worship: Its Theology and Practice*. 3rd ed. Nashville: Broadman and Holman, 2006.

For Specific Resources for Worship Technology:

Koster, Steven J. "Visual Media Technology in Christian Worship." Master's Thesis, Michigan State University, 2003.

Schultze, Quentin. *High-Tech Worship?: Using Presentational Technologies Wisely*. Grand Rapids: Baker, 2004.

Websites: "Technologies for Worship," http://tfwm.com/

Appendix B

DIAGRAM OF THE TEXT

The purpose of this exercise is to see the structure of the text.

• Place the independent clause at the left margin. • Place supporting words above or below the independent clause. • Designate the function of each phrase as it relates to the independent clause in the left column.	• Connect separated terms with lines as needed. • Mark significant theological terms. • Underline or highlight all verbs. Give emphasis to any imperatives.
Functions	**Diagram**

OBSERVATIONS OF THE TEXT

The purpose of this exercise is to work from diagram/structure of the text.

• Note observations verse by verse. • Focus on particular words/phrases.	• Consider this a brainstorming session.
Relationship of Text Ideas **Watch for** • Comparisons • Contrasts • Conditional statements • Correlative structure (either . . . or, neither . . . nor) • Reasons • Purpose • Results	
Significant Words **Watch for** • Theological themes • Figurative language • Repetition • Cross-references	
Rhetorical Functions **Watch for** • Assertions • Commands • Admonitions • Promises • Causes • Means • Agency	
Summaries • Summarize each theological theme • Show relationships between ideas, words, phrases	

SERMON OUTLINE

The purpose of this exercise is to create a sermon outline of the text from the Diagram and Observations made.

A. Foundational Elements

1. Sermon Title (in quotation marks; headline capitalization style):

2. Text:

3. Subject (in one or two words—or as a short phrase):

4. ETS (Essence of the Text in a Sentence—state in the past tense):

5. ESS (Essence of the Sermon in a Sentence—also called the Proposition; do not state in the past tense):

6. OSS (Objective of the Sermon in a Sentence—state in terms of what hearers will do as a result of this sermon): Hearers will. . .

B. Formal Elements

Introduction

1.
2.
3.

Body

I.
    1.
    2.
II.
    1.
    2.
III.
    1.
    2.

Conclusion

1.
2.
3.

C. Notes

1. The number of points may vary within the formal elements from the numbers shown above.

2. All main points (i.e., I, II, etc.) in the sermon body outline must be referenced to the text (e.g., I. The Motive of Salvation, John 3:16a; II. The Means of Salvation, John 3:16b).

3. Write all sermon body main points in headline capitalization style (e.g., The Motive of Salvation). Write all lesser points under the main points in sentence capitalization style (e.g., The personal motive).

Bibliography

"Tusculum Hills to House Bivocational/Small Church Center," SBC Life, September, 2014, accessed April 27, 2017, http://www.sbclife.net/Articles/2014/09/sla13.

Akin, Daniel L., Bill Curtis, and Stephen Rummage. *Engaging Exposition*. Nashville: B&H Academic, 2011.

Allen, David. *Preaching Tools: An Annotated Survey of Commentaries and Preaching Resources for Every Book of the Bible*. Fort Worth, TX: Seminary Hill Press, 2016.

Andrews, Edward D. *The Complete Guide to Bible Translation*. Cambridge, OH: Christian Publishing House, 2012.

Blanchard, Ken, Patricia Zigarmi, and Drea Zigarmi. *Leadership And The One-Minute Manager* New York, NY: William Morrow and Company, 1985.

Broadus, John A. *On the Preparation and Delivery of Sermons*, 4th ed., rev. Vernon L. Stanfield, 1870; revision, New York: Harper & Row, 1979.

Cathey, Bill. *A New Day in Church Revivals*. Nashville: Broadman Press, 1984.

Charles, H.B. *On Preaching: Personal & Pastoral Insights for the Preparation & Practice of Preaching*. Chicago: Moody, 2014.

Day, Bill. "Bivocational and Smaller Membership Church Council Report," www.sbc.net, June 14, 2016, accessed March 30, 2017, http://www.sbc.net/advisoryCouncilReports/pdf/Bivo-SmallChurch2016.pdf.

Dever, Mark, and Greg Gilbert. *Preach: Theology Meets Practice*. Nashville: B & H Publishing Group, 2012.

Fish, Roy. *Every Member Evangelism for Today*. New York: Harper and Row, 1976.

Ford, Leighton. *The Christian Persuader*. Philadelphia: Westminster Press, 1966.

Fullerton, W.Y. *Charles Haddon Spurgeon: A Bibliography*. CreateSpace Independent Publishing Platform, 2014.

Hull, Bill. *The Disciple Making Pastor*. Old Tappan, NJ: Fleming Revell, 1988.

Hull, Bill. *Conversion and Discipleship*. Grand Rapids, MI: Zondervan, 2016.

Hybels, Bill. *When Leadership and Discipleship Collide*. Grand Rapids, MI: Zondervan, 2006.

Johnston, Thomas. ed. Mobilizing a Great Commission Church for Harvest. Eugene: Wipf & Stock, 2011.

Kelley, Charles. *Adult Roman Road Witnessing Training Teacher's Guide*. Nashville: Home Mission Board of the Southern Baptist Convention, 1993.

Louisiana Baptist Convention. *One on One: Evangelism Made Simple*. Personal Evangelism Kit. Alexandria, La.: Evangelism/Church Growth Team, 2017.

Luter, Jr., Boyd. "Discipleship and the Church," *Bibliotheca Sacra Volume* 137 (1980).

MacArthur, John. *The Book on Leadership: The Power of a Godly Influence*. Nashville: T. Nelson Publishers, 2004.

Malphurs, Aubrey. *Being Leaders: The Nature of Authentic Christian Leadership*. Grand Rapids: Baker, 2003.

Malphurs, Aubrey. *Strategic Disciple Making*. Grand Rapids, MI: Baker Books, 2009.

McDill, Wayne. 12 *Essential Skills for Great Preaching*, 2d ed. revised and expanded. Nashville: B&H Publishing Group, 2006.

McKeever, Joe. "The Pastor Is the Worship Leader," accessed December 13, 2016, http://www.churchleaders.com/worship/worship-articles/177026-joe-mckeever-pastor-is-the-worship-leader.html?print .

North American Mission Board. *Revival Preparation Manual*. Atlanta: North American Mission Board, 2009.

North American Mission Board. 3 *Circles Evangelism Kit*. Atlanta: North American Mission Board, 2012

Packer, J.I. *Grounded in the Gospel*. Grand Rapids, MI: Baker Books, 2010.

Payne, J. D. *Pressure Points: Twelve Global Issues Shaping the Face of the Church*. Nashville: Thomas Nelson, 2013.

Peterson, Eugene. *A Long Obedience in the Same Direction*. Downers Grove, IL: IVP Books, 2010.

Piper, John. *What Jesus Demands from the World*. Wheaton, IL: Crossway, 2006.

Platt, David. *Radical: Taking Back Your Faith from the American Dream*. Colorado Springs, CO: Multnomah, 2010.

Rainer, Thom. *Effective Evangelistic Churches*. Nashville: Broadman and Holman Publishers, 1996.

Rainer, Thom. *The Bridger Generation*. Nashville: Broadman and Holman, 1997.

Readings, Leah. "10 Church Technology Stats that will Astound You," Capterra, accessed December 15, 2016, http://blog.capterra.com/church-technology-stats/.

Reid, Alvin. *Evangelism Handbook*. Nashville: B&H Publishing Group, 2009.

Robinson, Haddon. *Biblical Preaching: The Development and Delivery of Expository Messages*. Grand Rapids: Baker Book House, 1980.

Roudkovski, Jake. "An Investigation into a Relationship between Pastoral Personal Evangelism and Baptisms in Selected Southern Baptist Churches." Ph.D. diss., New Orleans Baptist Theological Seminary, 2004.

Scazzero, Peter. *The Emotionally Healthy Leader: How Transforming Your Inner Life Will Deeply Transform Your Church, Team, and the World*. Grand Rapids, Michigan: Zondervan, 2015.

Sills, David. *Changing World, Unchanging Mission: Responding to Global Challenges*. Downers Grove, IL: IVP, 2015.

Spurgeon, Charles. *Lectures to My Students*. Grand Rapids: Zondervan, 1954.

Spurgeon, Charles H. *Spurgeon at His Best*, compiled by Tom Carter. Grand Rapids, MI: Baker, 1991.

Steele, Ed. *Worship HeartCries: Personal Preparation for Corporate Worship*. North Charleston, SC: CreateSpace Independent Publishing Platform, 2013.

Streett, Alan. *The Effective Invitation*. Grand Rapids: Kregel, 1995.

Vaters, Karl. "The Grasshopper Myth," "Pivot, accessed April 14, 2017, http://www. christianitytoday.com/karl-vaters/about/books.html?paging=off.

Vines, Jerry and Jim Shaddix. *Power in the Pulpit*. Chicago: Moody Press, 1997.

Waggoner, Brad J. *The Shape of Faith to Come*. Nashville, TN: Broadman & Holman Publishing Group, 2008.

Welch, Robert H. *Church Administration: Creating Efficiency for Effective Ministry*, 2nd ed. Nashville: B&H Academic, 2001.

Whitney, Donald S. *Spiritual Disciplines for the Christian Life*, revised and updated. ed. Colorado Springs: NavPress, 2014.

Willard, Dallas. *The Spirit of the Disciplines: Understanding How God Changes Lives*. San Francisco: Harper & Row, 1988.

Willard, Dallas. *The Great Omission: Reclaiming Jesus's Essential Teachings on Discipleship*. New York, NY: HarperCollins, 2006.

Wittstock, Peter. *Hear Him! The One Hundred and Twenty Five Commands of Jesus*. Longwood, FL: Xulon Press, 2004.